Investing and trading 2 in 1

Contents

Chapter 29 You should also plan on setting a "Stop loss price," too. This is a protective move to make sure you don't get badly burned by the stock price moving in the wrong direction. Let's say you've bought shares of XYZ Corporation when their price was at $4.50 a share. Based on your research, you expect an upward move by the share price and plan on selling when it reaches $4.75 a share (always have an exit price planned). Then something goes wrong. Bad news upsets the market (in general or it effects your stock in particular), and your stock price starts dropping instead. Wisely, you left a stop loss order with your broker, in effect instructing the broker to automatically sell your shares when their price drops to a certain point (perhaps in this example $4.35) to limit your loss. You should know that stop loss orders aren't foolproof. Your broker still must find someone to buy the shares at that point. In times of crisis, share prices can fall so fast that they blow by the stop loss price and keep going before they finally sell, making your loss bigger than anticipated. While this isn't a regular occurrence, unexpected events can cause them. The company selling the Epipen recently saw its valuation drop $3 billion dollars in a short period of time because of news about its price markup. No day trader could have anticipated this news, and even with stop loss

Introduction

There is a very strong belief that day trading is a hard skill to master, which is not necessarily the case. It may be tough at the beginning but it gets better as you go on mastering the skills and gaining experience. Many people have tried it in the past and probably failed in it because they did not take time to learn the necessary skills and to acquire the most required experience to trade successfully. Trading like an expert will take time but this does not mean that a new day trader will not make it.

There are many things that come into play for one to day trade successfully, and one of them is changing the way one thinks. One should be aware of how they have been programmed to think, and with the information out there about day trading and the stock market, you can easily change your thinking in order to grasp a trading opportunity for a profit.

Planning is another thing that traders need to embrace in order to trade successfully. Many traders have the belief that trading more amounts to more profits which is not always the case with day trading. A plan will help you concentrate on quality trades and not on quantity trades, with the former more beneficial than the latter.

Above all, learn as much as you can. There is a lot of information out there that you can take advantage of. Information is power and this will help you to trade successfully at all times.

Rules of Day Trading

Let's turn our focus to some of the rules of day trading that every investor should follow. These rules are not necessarily set in stone. You can decide to take these rules with you on your investing journey or ignore them. However, they should be followed in order to give you the best day trading experience from the very first day of your investing career.

Day Trading is a Serious Business

When some people start day trading, they think that it's meant to be fun and games and don't take the profession seriously. This can be a grave mistake. While you want to enjoy what you are doing, you always want to remember that it is a serious business.

There are some types of investing that are easier to handle as a side career or on the weekends. If this is the type of investing you are looking for, you will not want to look at day trading. This type of investing is meant to be a daily business and many people look at it as their day job. This means that once you decide to become a day trader officially, you need to treat it as you would any other career. You have to get up in the morning, get ready for your day, and make sure you are ready to work by your set time, which could be as early as 7 in the morning.

While you will have some flexibility in your schedule from a regular job, meaning you could set a bit of a later start time in the morning, you will want to make sure to set a schedule you will follow at least Monday through Friday. Even working from home, you will want to make sure to limit distractions. For example, you won't want to focus on day trading and watching television at the same time. Set up an office for yourself and pay attention to your work. Get ready for your job as a day trader like you would for your job at any other office. Don't head into your office in your pajamas. You're more likely to feel like you want to put in 100% effort and succeed if you treat this as a career.

Day Trading Will Not Help You Get Rich Quickly
You should not look at day trading as a get rich quick arrangement. This is a common misconception and one reason people often turn to day trading. If you truly want to become a successful day trader, you will need to make sure you not only have the patience to build your investments, but also realize it takes time.

Day Trader is Harder Than it Looks
Day trading is not as easy as it looks, but this does not mean that you should set this book down and decide not to become a day trader. It just means that you will probably need to spend more time learning about day trading than you initially thought. You want to make sure you are well-versed in the field before you make your first investment. Luckily for you, this is one of the reasons I decided to write this book.

I want to give you a comprehensive beginner's guide so you can learn as much as you can about day trading to start your journey in one location. In other words, I have done most of the research for you.

Trading is Different from Investing

One of the biggest rules that you should understand before becoming a day trader is this is different from investing. In order to help you understand the difference, here are a few basic differences between trading and investing:

As an investor, you need to have an idea where the stocks are heading in the future. However, as a day trader, you only need to concern yourself with which stocks will give you the best financial gain on that day. You look more closely at the minutes. In fact, you won't even pay much attention to the hours and definitely won't worry about the next day, week, month, or year.

You Won't Win Every Trade

It does not matter how experienced you become as a day trader, there will still be days that you lose on a trade. Many people create an image in their mind where they will become so experienced at trading that they will never make a mistake and they will only gain capital.

The trick to help you lose as little capital as possible when you lose on a trade is to follow the various risk management strategies. I will discuss several risk management strategies later in this book.

Chapter 1 Day Trading Basics

It's time for you to take a look at the day trading process works. You could just blindly jump in, but that's a recipe for disaster. Instead, let's get you started on how to smartly engage in day trading.

The first question to ask yourself is how big an investment are you planning on making in your day trading efforts? You need to consider not only how much money you're willing to invest, but also how much time. Many investors look at day trading as an escape from their normal jobs, others see it as an answer to the uncertainties of the job market. While you may hunger to day trade full time, people do succeed as part time day traders while working a primary job. Beginners may also want to spend some time simulating investments to get a feel for how comfortable you are with the process and how much talent you may have. As mentioned in the last paragraph, simply jumping in is not a good idea. You need to understand the investment market, learn to look for indicators that give you an idea of stock movements, and make the most of your opportunities.

Infrastructure Concerns

While it may sound mundane, spending some time on your workspace and technology can be well worth it. Day trading can definitely be stressful, so a work area that provides quiet and privacy can be helpful. Don't underestimate the importance of a reliable Internet connection and a backup method of controlling your investments in case your network goes down. These days it's not hard to have a fast land based Internet connection while also having the ability to use your smartphone as a wireless hotspot if your main connection goes down. It only takes one network failure when you have a big investment on the line, to convince you of the importance of a backup Internet access plan.

Understanding the Market

It's one thing to say you want to invest in stocks. It's another thing to figure out what stocks you should be investing in. Investors break down the market into different sectors such as "retailers," "manufacturers," "utilities," "airlines," "energy," "health care," and others. Day traders can choose to target all these sectors or choose to specialize in one or more. As a beginner, focusing on one sector may be advantageous, particularly if it's one you're already familiar with.

Since as a day trader, you're interested in identifying opportunities for small, changes in stocks, not long-term growth. This means you'll need ample funding. U.S. based day traders need a minimum of $25,000 for their trading account, according to Securities and Exchange Commission (SEC) rules. This means you'd really need at least $30,000 to have some flexibility. Keep in mind; in the U.S. you can currently leverage your trading capital up to 400%. This means that you could control $120,000 worth of stock with your $30,000. As you learned earlier, this also means you could suffer four times the losses on your investments. Be aware too, that if you don't maintain your maintenance margin amount, you can receive a margin call. In planning for your trading account, it would be better to have more funds available, since that would make more stocks available for your consideration. Remember too, it's usually more cost efficient to buy shares in multiples of 100, meaning a small investment kitty will either limit you to cheaply priced stocks or buying stocks in smaller increments than are less cost effective. If you can devote more funds to your trading account, you'll be able to pursue more opportunities, and have the wherewithal to recover from losses.

Calculating a Simple Moving Average

The moving average is a basic tool investor use to monitor a stock's behavior over a defined period of time. The investor simply adds the stock's closing price for a specific period of time (two weeks, a month, a quarter, etc.) and then divides that number by the number of trading days in that period. A trader will calculate a short-term moving average and a long-term moving average for a stock (actually, you'll probably calculate a few more than this to get a better sense of the stock's behavior). A simple moving average can tell you whether a stock is on a rising or declining trend.

An important point for many traders is when the short term moving average rises above or below the long-term moving average. A short-term moving average that crosses above a long-term moving average often indicates the stock is about to begin an upward trend. The opposite is also true.

One approach to using moving averages compares a specific short-term moving average (50 days) with a specific long-term moving average (200 days). If the 50-day average moves below the 200 day average, you have a bearish signal. This is known as a "Death Cross." If the 50 average moves above the 200-day average, it is a bullish signal, and is known as a "Golden Cross." While it would be nice if you could rely solely on such a simple system, remember that relying only on a moving average approach is unreliable. It's better to use this information as another bit of information when making your trading plans.

Choosing a Broker

Once you've decided on your trading allocation, you need to choose a broker or brokerage. There are a number of online discount brokers available to the novice investor. Many will offer you their own electronic trading program. Don't be surprised to get offers for free trades and a bonus for picking their firm. Free trades and cash bonuses are nice, but make sure you choose a broker you feel comfortable with and one that checks out with your research.

The biggest online brokerages include: TD Ameritrade, Scott Trade, Fidelity Brokerage, Charles Schwab, Options Express, Merrill Edge, Robinhood, Loyal3, Options House, EOption, and others. Some like Robinhood offer free trades, making their overhead on charging interest on margin accounts and using customer cash to earn interest. Others may offer more services or access to more investment exchanges. One thing you won't get from any of these discount brokerages though is personal advice. That's the purview of the traditional broker.

In choosing a brokerage, consider the cost of trades, your comfort level with its trading program, and your ability to access the company's website. Also, look into what others are saying about the brokerage and whether or not it handles the investment vehicles you're interested in trading.

Buy Orders, Sell Orders, and Setting a Stop Loss Price

Not every move a trader makes has to be executed immediately or at random. You can tell your brokerage you only want to buy or sell a stock when it hits a certain price. The risk of course, is that the stock may not hit that price while you have money planned for it.

You should also plan on setting a "Stop loss price," too. This is a protective move to make sure you don't get badly burned by the stock price moving in the wrong direction. Let's say you've bought shares of XYZ Corporation when their price was at $4.50 a share. Based on your research, you expect an upward move by the share price and plan on selling when it reaches $4.75 a share (always have an exit price planned). Then something goes wrong. Bad news upsets the market (in general or it effects your stock in particular), and your stock price starts dropping instead. Wisely, you left a stop loss order with your broker, in effect instructing the broker to automatically sell your shares when their price drops to a certain point (perhaps in this example $4.35) to limit your loss. You should know that stop loss orders aren't foolproof. Your broker still has to find someone to buy the shares at that point. In times of crisis, share prices can fall so fast that they blow by the stop loss price and keep going before they finally sell, making your loss bigger than anticipated. While this isn't a regular occurrence, unexpected events can cause them. The company selling the Epi-pen recently saw it's valuation drop $3 billion dollars in a short period of time because of news about its price markup. No day trader could have anticipated this news, and even with stop loss orders, traders who were expecting upward movement in this stock, probably lost more than they expected.

Chapter 2 Choosing Which Stocks to Trade

Now that you have established your trading plan, you can start your research on which securities you will trade with it. There are several different securities that can be traded with a day trading method, including stocks, currencies, options, ETFs and mutual funds. All of these trade differently and having an understanding of how each behaves in the marketplace is critical before beginning trading. Here, we will focus mainly on stocks, as they are a very common security for day trading.

There are literally thousands of stocks available for trade on any given day, and each moves within the market uniquely. How do you decide which stock or stocks to trade? Do you simply go after the most popular and widely traded like Google and Apple? Or do you just go after IPOs and hope for a quick flip? Finding the best stocks to trade based on your methodology is going to require a bit of research. The following steps will help you through it:

Create your watch list

Since there are so many stocks to trade, you can't possibly watch them all on a daily basis. Before you really get going, create a list of stocks whose movements you can monitor. It is best to choose one or two sectors then choose a few stocks from each to put on your watch list. Some of the most popular sectors are:

- Banking

- Precious Metals

- Semiconductor

- Automotive

- Pharmaceuticals

- Retail

- Internet

Choose one or two sectors that you would like to follow then track the movement of the top issues. Limit the number of stocks that you follow to about 10 per sector, maxing out at 20 stocks being monitored at a time. This will allow you to truly track and understand their movement trends.

Get an early start on Trading Day

Day trading is not going to be conducive to flopping into your desk chair 10 minutes before the market opens. The market moves fast and you need to have your day plan established before it opens. Getting started early, at least an hour or two before market open, gives you an opportunity to do your research and configure your monitors with the stocks you will trade that day.

Once you have your cup of coffee and have settled into your desk, begin to analyze the pre-market. If you've been involved in the market for a while, you know not to place any gambles based solely on pre-market movement, as the swings can be drastic. However, doing a scan will give you a place to start when choosing which stocks to work with that day. Here is a guideline for what to look for:

1. Stocks priced over $5. If you have placed tight stops on your plan (and you should have), stocks that are priced below this mark will not give you much wiggle room during the trade.

2. Look for stocks with somewhat heavy volume. A stock may show that it is up 25%, but if it's only on 200 shares, you should move right along.

3. Once you have found a stock in the correct price range that is positive on a reasonable volume, review the volume average over the last 30 days. This will give

you an idea of how the stock usually trades and whether it is a good candidate for day trading.

At this point, you will also want to review the broad market for the major indices.

Trade High Volume Stocks

It is advisable to trade on stocks that have a high enough volume that you can quickly enter and exit trades. Your brokerage account will likely provide a "most active" list which will give you the top 10 or 20 highest volume stocks; that is a great place to start. Finding a screener that will go beyond this ranking, though, will be advantageous as it will allow you a broader list and possibly stocks that are not being tracked by every investor. It is also a good idea to look at stocks that are rising on high volume relative to themselves. If a stock usually trades 3 million shares per day, but today has 5 million shares traded by market open, this is certainly something worth exploring.

Monitor the Earnings Calendar

Before delving any further into this, be advised that it is very *ill-advised* to place trades before earnings are posted. Pre-positioning yourself for earnings announcements is just another form of gambling. Reporting of earnings, however, is one event that increases volatility and knowing who will be reporting that week gives you an idea of who the likely movers will be.

Check out Social Media

Social Media has crept into so many aspects of all of our lives, why not investment strategy as well? There are now social media streams that will give you another method for scanning the market. *StockTwits* and *StockCharts* are two forums that stream real-time information on which stocks are being discussed and which charts are being monitored. This could give you an idea of market movement that other traders are seeing first. Be careful when making decisions using these platforms, however, since you don't always know the validity of the sources. They would be best regarded as a jumping off point for doing your own research.

A final word on choosing stocks: If the above seems like a lot of work (because it is) and you would rather master something a little more simple, consider trading the same one or two stocks every day and learn to understand their movements. You could simply choose one of the most popular stocks with a lot of volume (like Google or Apple). This will be a little less stressful than reacting daily to market action and allows you to learn the trading pattern and identify the technical indicators for that particular security.

Overall, for a day trader the two most important qualities in a stock are liquidity and volatility. Tight spreads with low slippage (the difference between the expected price of a stock and the actual price), combined with the right amount of volatility create the perfect environment for lucrative trading.

Chapter 3 Tools and Platforms

Get Your Education

You need to make sure you are educated on your topic. You want to treat day trading as your new career. Therefore, you should make sure that you have researched your topic and consider yourself an expert on day trading. Of course, there are lessons that you are going to learn naturally as you start day trading. Experienced traders believe that people should take about three to four months and practice with simulators before practicing with money.

Build Your Business Plan

You need to have a business plan. One of the biggest factors to remember when you are getting into day trading is you have to treat it like any other serious career choice. With any business you would start up and get into, you will have a business plan. You need to make sure your education is part of your business plan (for example, any classes you are planning on taking). You also have to make sure your schedule, the tools you will use, platforms, technology, software, and anything else incorporated in your business is a part of your business plan.

Another thing to remember when creating your business plan is to look at every single detail. You do not want to miss something or think it is fine to skip over anything. On top of this, you want to make sure that you look at your business plan often, even after you start trading. In fact, it is best if you look at your business plan at least once a month, if not more.

Make Sure You Have the Right Supplies

You will want to make sure that you find a system of support from a community of traders, have high-speed internet service, a great platform which supports hotkeys, a scanner which will help you find the right stocks to trade, and the best broker. You will also want to make sure that you can financially handle the bills that will become a part of your new day trading career. These bills can include leases and licenses for software, your monthly internet bill, electricity bill, your broker's commission, and any platform costs. Furthermore, you will probably want to become a part of an online community, a practice that has several benefits I will discuss later in his book, and bear in mind that these communities often have subscriptions.

Have Enough Cash

You will need to make sure that you have enough cash, which is often referred to as startup capital. Similar to any other business, you will want to make sure you can afford to take on day trading. However, you will not only need money when you start investing, you will also need money to make sure that you can afford the bills and technology that goes into day trading, as mentioned earlier.

Making sure you have enough finances is an important step because one of the main reasons why most day traders lose their money or go bankrupt is because they didn't have enough startup capital. If you need to hold off on starting up your day trading career for a couple of months or more in order to make sure you have enough capital, that is okay. As the old saying goes, it is better to be safe than sorry. You don't want to find yourself thinking of ways to cut back in order to save your money for investing. For example, it is a bad idea to decide not to go forth with any classes or day-trading community subscriptions over financial concerns, as these are incredibly important. If you start cutting back on the tools that can help you become a successful day trader, you can easily find yourself in a downward spiral. This can cause you not only to lose more money but also cause you a lot of stress and emotions within trading, which can cause more problems within your investing career by impairing your ability to make quick decisions based on logical analysis. If you are not prepared, you are more likely to make mistakes.

Find a Broker

One of the first things you will want to do is to find a trusted broker. It is important that you not only find a capable, competent broker but one whom you can trust. Remember, you will be getting assistance from your broker about your financial future. Therefore, you will want to make sure that you not only talk to the broker before you agree to hire, but you will also want to take extra steps in checking into your broker's background. You have the right to find out how your broker has handled other people's accounts. For example, background information can tell you about any complaints people have filed against the broker previously. On top of this, you will be able to see your broker's employment history and get an idea of why the broker changed jobs in the past.

The broker you pick will help you with many tasks. Not only with they give you advice on which stocks to pick but they might also go through with the buying and selling process of the stocks. The best brokers will work with you and help you learn the trade. If you find that your broker is withholding information of any type, such as not giving you the correct information about stocks or not allowing you to see your records, you need to find a different broker. You always have the right to see all your records and know exactly what your broker is doing with your stocks and finances.

Know Your Rights
Before you search for your trusted broker, there are several pieces of information you should know first. One of these is your rights when it comes to working with a broker.

• You have the right to ask for and receive information about your broker's background. This can help you get to know your broker, so you can find one that you can trust with your personal information and finances.

• You have the right to know all the information about any stocks or trades before your broker makes any purchase or sale.

• You have the right to all reports about your trading.

• You have the right to ask any questions or seek any other means to help you understand all the reports and information you are given.

• You have the right to receive all forms of communication in the form of letters or other means of written correspondence. No one has any right to keep you from seeing and understanding any of your information.

- If you do not feel that you are receiving all your information, you do not understand your reports, or you do not feel your broker is helping, you have the right to go above your broker to his or her supervisor.

- If your broker is part of a branch firm, you have the right to go to the branch firm's headquarters with any questions or concerns.

- You have the right to contact your state or county agency with any concerns about your broker's background, including employment history or any complaints filed against your broker.

Types of Brokers

1. Sure Trader is a broker who focuses on international trades. Sure Traders also tend to focus on helping the day traders who do not fall under the $25,000 minimum rule for United States residents. This rule is known as the pattern day trader rule set up by the Financial Industry Regulatory Authority. This rule states that not only must the day trader maintain a $25,000 minimum balance in his account, but the customer must also make at least four trades during a five day period.

While Sure Traders are common for day traders, not all traders, especially when they first begin trading, can hold the minimum amount in their account. It is also important to note that these brokers have higher fees. For example, their commissions are usually higher, such as charging over $10 for one buy and sell trade. At the same time, Sure Traders are the best choice for people who cannot keep the minimum balance in their accounts.

2. Interactive Brokers tend to be one of the cheapest types of brokers, as they only charge about $1 per trade. However, they generally won't work with people who can't follow the pattern day trader rule. If you are a day trader who is planning on purchasing thousands of shares, this is the best type of broker for you because their fees are the lowest. However, you will want to make sure that you can follow the rule and have some experience in day trading. The more stocks you purchase, the more experienced you should be. It is fine to just start with a few stocks while you are still learning the ropes of day trading. This will

help you limit mistakes and minimize risk. The more stocks you purchase, the more risk you have.

No matter what your conditions are, you always need to make sure that you find the right broker for you. Furthermore, you have to make sure that you can trust your broker. If you don't have a good relationship with your broker or you find yourself wondering if your broker is really helping you, it is time to take whatever steps you need to in order to secure your financial future.

Chapter 4 Calculating Risk vs Reward

So how do you create a plan? In essence, a plan will tell you when exactly you should stop the trade to cut losses or add to a position. When you should exit a trade to lock in profit or size down on a position. As with each trade, you always want to have a favorable risk vs reward ratio of at least 3:1. Risk vs reward ratio can be determined from support and resistance lines. It means that if you enter a trade with a stock price of $6 and you are willing to risk a loss of $1, you should always make sure that the chart is set up for a potential reward of $3. This is a simple rule of thumb which I govern all of my trades.

In the chart of COUP below, you can see that at 9.00am, if I want to enter a short position at $9.80, I will base my risk at $10.00, which is the short-term top and line of support. If the chart ramps over $10.00 afterwards, I will cut my loss immediately. That is a plan.

Cutting Losses

Cutting losses has always been one of my top rules when I day trade. A lot of traders refuse to cut losses because they BELIEVE that the stock will rebound. When you are trading, never allow yourself to lose more than you win, and to do that, you should always cut your losses decisively. You can always enter the market again when the chart set itself up, but you can never take back the money you have just lost.

How to Determine a Strong Resistance or Support Line?

A strong support or resistance line is one that has been tested by the chart many times but never been successfully broken out of. A strong line of support or resistance usually provides a better and more accurate gauge for risk or reward because every time the chart goes near this line, the crowd believes that the line will serve as the support or resistance yet again and react accordingly. This becomes a very strong self-fulfilling prophecy. It is also useful to note that if the chart breaks out of a strong line of support or resistance, it will typically experience a strong move in the direction of its breakout. When trading a stock, it is important to look at both the daily and intraday chart to identify if such a line exists in the 3-6month time frames. If it exists, you should respect this strong line of support/resistance when trading the intraday chart and plan your risk versus reward accordingly.

Whole Number Psychology

Paying attention to whole number marks also helps in gauging the risk versus reward for a trade. Many traders pay attention to whole dollar marks ($10.00) or half dollar marks ($10.50) more closely. For example, if the stock is currently priced at $9.64 intraday and trending higher, many traders will believe that it can push towards $10.00 and buy into it. Once the stock hits $10.00, everybody will be thinking of taking profits and sell off. At this point, the $10.00 mark is acting as a psychological line of resistance. It is always wise to pay attention to this whole and half dollar mark when you are trading and make plans based off these numbers.

Chapter 5 Trading Options

What are options?

Options are a popular instrument that is used in the stock market. Options are a great choice for beginners, as it will help them understand how the stock market works. Options are security instruments that are easy to trade in. You don't have to go the lengths that you have to trade in stocks and can easily buy and sell options. Let us look at examples to understand the concept better.

Suppose there is a television for sale and it is being sold at a reasonable price. You plan to buy it but will not be able to pay the full price for it. Instead, you will pay a little towards it as an advance and reserve it. You will promise to pay the remainder in say a week's time. The seller will agree and promise not to give the television to anyone. During the following week, you will find out that the television actually belonged to a very famous personality and you got it at a very reasonable price. If you were to sell it now with the information that you have received, then you stand to earn quite a lot of money from it. You then quickly pay for the television and buy it and then sell it for a higher price. The seller will have to give it to you at the agreed price as he has promised you the same and cannot go back on his promise.

On the other hand, if during the week you find out that the television is very old and useless and you have been overcharged for it then you have an option to refuse its purchase. You can call the seller and tell him that you changed your mind about it and don't want the television anymore. But, you will have to part with the advance money that you paid for it.

That was a general example let us look at a specific one now.

Now say you are offered 100 shares at $20 each. You will have to pay $2000 to acquire it. You pay the trader $500 for it and reserve it. Now during the week, you find out that the stocks are actually great investments and will help you earn you much more than what you have spent on it. You can immediately pay the difference and then sell them to another person for $60 each thereby earning a profit of $10 per share. The seller will be obligated to give the stocks to you at the agreed price and cannot ask you for anymore.

However, if during the week you find out that the stocks belong to a bad company and are being over-priced then you have the chance to refuse them. You can state that they are now valued at $40 each, which will cause you to undergo a loss. You will be saving $1500 in the process.

But you will have to part with the $500 that you paid as advance towards it. This is seen as a good deal as you will manage to save the bigger amount and part with only a little money that is paid as advance.

When such a deal happens, the seller will always want the price to fall and the buyer will want the price to rise.

Many types' securities can be traded as options. The underlying security should be stated when you get into the deal so that you can do a research on the same.

What are their types?

Options can be of two main types, American options and European options. You have to understand these in order to deal in them.

American options

America options refer to those that can be exchanged at any time even before the maturity or the expiry date of the options. Say for example you bought an option in May 2016 and it will mature in May 2017. If in December, you have the chance to sell the option and attain a profit from it then you can sell it freely. These form the most issued types of options.

European options

These form the other types of options that are issued. European options unlike American options will not allow you to sell them any time. You have to wait until they mature in order to do so. Even if it proves to be a good option to sell them in between, you will not be able to do so. This type is not popular anymore and is generally avoided by most traders.

Note that these are just names of the options and have no geographic relevance.

Concepts of options

These are the different concepts of options.

Call option

The call option refers to the option to buy assets at an agreed price on or prior to a particular date. The date is agreed upon by the buyer and the seller. Generally, the seller has a say in it, as he will be looking to profit from the deal. During the sale period, the buyer will hope for the price to rise so that he can get a good deal out of it.

Put option

The put option is the opposite of the call option. It refers to the option to sell certain assets at an agreed price on a chosen date. Here, the seller will hope for the price of the stock to drop so that the buyer will refuse to buy it and he will be left with the money paid as advance.

These form the different concepts of options.

Intraday Patterns

Bull Flags

Bull Flags on the intraday chart are much different than on the daily chart because they usually form so much tighter. You can have 3 basic types of bull flags. All consist of a flag pole then either a falling wedge, triangle wedge or flag formation. Bear/Bull flags offer day traders the best risk:reward.

Requirements

- Flag Pole

This is the "Rip Stick or Rip Sticks" that are the jolt or majority of the move that would be the most parabolic.

- Flag

This is either a falling wedge, flag formation or triangle wedge.

- High volume spike at the flag pole and decreasing volume during the flag.

This will often appear like a huge spike in volume then a "stair step down" in volume. It does not always have the stair step down, but you just want to make sure that the "consolidation period" has much less volume than the initial rip higher. If you get a random volume spike that is very large while the flag is taking shape, especially if it red, THIS WILL NEGATE THE PATTERN. Intraday is a little trickier than a typical flag on the daily because you will want to determine what time frame is in play. The 5 minute may have a flag, but switching to a 15 minute may "clear up" any mess on the chart or sloppy volume that you see in the pattern.

- Apex Point or resolution point on falling wedges, or triangle wedges.
- Unlike a daily pattern; on an awesome flag pattern intraday I do like to see a spike in volume. You may not always get one, but you have confidence to add to your position when you do.

Understand

- The tighter the flag the better the chance it resolves in your favor. I am going to get into determining your target in the protective theory section because this can differ from the daily patterns even though the same rule applies with using the flag pole at the break.

Flags can resolve before or after the Apex point. The Apex point is used a general guide and brings the time element into the trade. The bigger the flag pole (or larger the initial move) the longer it may take for the flag to resolve.

OLED Bull Flag Triangle Wedge

This is an awesome bull flag and I am going to go over some points here in this example that is very important. First, algos are color blind to patterns. Even though you have a high initial red spike you will see that the shape still took a flag formation to a triangle wedge. Second, it is very common to get a retest of the flag in bull or bear cases. In this particular case you broke out from the flag at 35.75 and ran to 36.50 before retesting the flag pattern. Hopefully you would have locked in gains had you played this one.

ENDP 5 Minute Chart / Random Red Volume Spikes

I put the 5 minute chart of ENDP on here to show you the volume, but the 15 minute chart was actually the chart in play. If you look at the volume you will notice the 2 big red spikes and the stock failed to resolve bullishly. This is also an example of a 5 minute speed line break going into lunch where the flag failed to resolve. This stock went 7 bars in the pattern with a weak breakout which is what we talked about on determining what time frame to play. And yes.... Algos are still color blind, but when you get these big spikes during digestion when you are not at the APEX point, that is bad news.

Bear Flags

Bear Flags on the intraday chart are much different than on the daily chart because they usually form so much tighter. You can have 3 basic types of bear flags. All consist of a flag pole then either a rising wedge, triangle wedge or flag formation. Bear/Bull flags offer day traders the best risk:reward.

Requirements

- Flag Pole

This is the "Rip Stick or Rip Sticks" that are the jolt or majority of the move that would be the most parabolic.

- Flag

This is either a rising wedge, flag formation or triangle wedge.

- High volume spike at the flag pole and decreasing volume during the flag.

This will often appear like a huge spike in volume then a "stair step down" in volume. It does not always have the stair step down, but you just want to make sure that the "consolidation period" has much less volume than the initial rip higher. If you get a random volume spike that is very large while the flag is taking shape, especially if it is green THIS WILL NEGATE THE PATTERN. Intraday is a little trickier than a typical flag on the daily because you will want to determine what time frame is in play. The 5 minute may have a flag, but switching to a 15 minute may "clear up" any mess on the chart or sloppy volume that you see in the pattern.

- Apex Point or resolution point on falling wedges, or triangle wedges.
- Unlike a daily pattern on an awesome flag pattern, intraday I do like to see a spike in volume. You may not always get one, but you have confidence to add to your position when you do.

Understand

- The tighter the flag the better the chance it resolves in your favor. I am going to get into determining your target in the protective theory section because this can differ from the daily patterns even though the same rule applies with using the flag pole at the break.
- Flags can resolve before or after the Apex point. The Apex point is used as a general guide and brings the time element into the trade. The bigger the flag pole (or larger the initial move) the longer it may take for the flag to resolve

SWI Triangle Wedge 5 Minute Bear Flag

You can see the huge rip down consisted of above average volume forming the flag pole. Then you will see the triangle wedge drawn in white lines around the flag and consolidated volume as the flag was forming. The most critical thing here that allowed this stock to drop from 34.30 to 32.84 was volume on the break which would be the point where you would double up. Risk is best when you enter during the pattern formation near the apex point at the top of the flag.

Falling Wedge
HALO 5 Minute Flag

A falling wedge is different than the daily because it is not a line sloping down for the support line. Typically the stock will find a base and test that multiple times with a triangle top. The daily chart remember had both lines sloping down, but the resistance line sloped down much more than the support line. Intraday the best falling wedge patterns have a base like the one below. Also to play a rising wedge or a falling wedge *YOU MUST HAVE A FLAG POLE ON AN INTRADAY CHART!* This is not true with a daily chart.

Rising Wedge/ Rising Wedge Flag
NFLX 5 Minute Rising Wedge Bear Flag

A rising wedge intraday is different than the daily because it is a continuation pattern. This can have 2 highs that form a horizontal line that don't make a higher high for the top part of the flag, or it can be like the example below which is very common. Remember you must have a flag pole in order to play these intraday. You want a big spike in volume, then you want consolidated volume during the form of the flag and preferably a volume spike on the break. *FLAG POLE IS A MUST!*

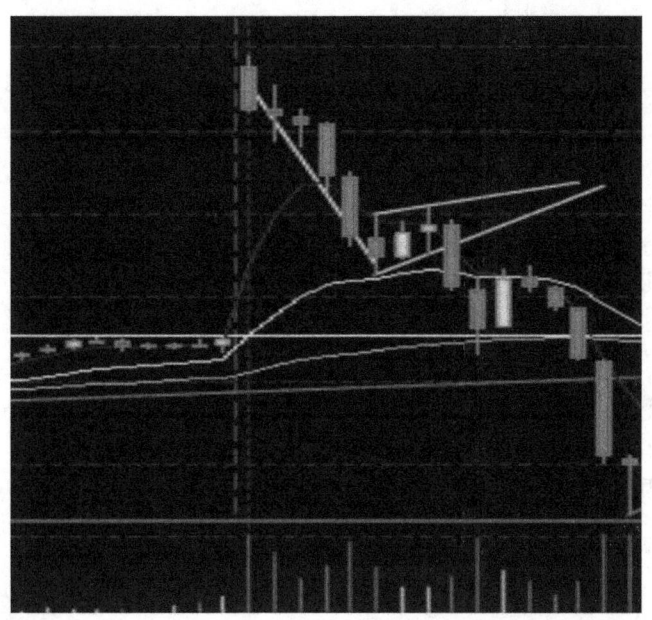

Advanced VWAP trading setups

VWAP is volume based and volume is the number one factor influencing tradable price action. Trading the VWAP is a high technical strategy developed to minimize risk parameters while maximizing profit potential. As intraday traders, our number one concern is risk and how to minimize it, so before entering any trade you should be asking yourself the question, "What's the risk involved?"

It is important to avoid lunch hour trades during 12-1:30 pm EST because during that time period the volume is much lighter, and the market is chopper, thus making it much harder to make a trade successfully, so in the long run, avoiding this time period will benefit you.

Three common VWAP setups

VWAP Pop-A bullish, long based trade

VWAP Crack- A bearish, short based trade

VWAP Fade- A bearish, short based trade

The tools for VWAP strategies

1. A Stock In Play!

Definition: A stock in play is defined as any stock trading at an extreme, or, far outside its normal range on high relative volume- all fueled by a catalyst.

2. VWAP

3. 9 EMA

4. 20 EMA

VWAP pop: the price action comes off the bottom, clears through VWAP and continues on to the highs.

Setup

A stock in play must comes up and clears through VWAP, 9 and 20 EMA's

Allow a 5 minutes decision candle to become established.

The decision candle must have broken through and *closed above* VWAP and will now act as your initiation trigger and your risk factors (AKA stop).

Initiating a position

Begin to establish a long position as the price action clears the high of the decision candle. So remember the decision candle is the candle that comes up of the bottom and clears through 9, 20 EMA as well as VWAP and closes above VWAP. *It is very important that the candle closes above VWAP.* So once the price action clears through the high of that decision candle, you would want to get in long. Now you have to determine your stop and stop would be determined by the low of the decision candle. Based on your stop, you would want to size up your position correctly to meet your risk parameters. To summarize, the initiation trigger is the high of the decision candle and stop out point is the low of the decision candle. As the move starts to confirm which means price action establishes a pivot point and begins to move away from VWAP, we can start to add to our position. Once we have added to our position, we can move our stops higher to the candle that makes the move through the decision candle. We will get into real life examples after I discuss about the sell targets.

Predetermine sell target

Your first sell target should be the next clearest point of resistance, or, at least at a point that meets a 2:1 reward/risk ratio which means your profit target has to be at least two times the distance from your entry to your stop. *Always use the 9 EMA and 5 mins candle close below that as your indicator for further reduction or close of your position.* I like to take some profits once it hit the 2:1 reward/risk target, then I like to use the 9 EMA as a momentum indictor, as long as the price action can stay above the 9 EMA, I will continue to be long in the trade. The exit point will be a 5 minutes candle close below 9 EMA, and that is when you can reduce more of your position if not all of them. After reducing more of the position, I may keep a last piece on depending on how far in green I am and I will trail the balance of the position using higher lows/pivot points.

Now let's take a look at a VWAP pop trade on $ORCL

The green line on my chart is the VWAP. Blue line is the 9 EMA and the gray line is the 20 EMA. The stock was in play because it has earnings out (catalyst). We can see, as the price action began to move off the bottom and it cleared through first the 9 EMA, then the 20 EMA and it closed above VWAP. Once we got that 5 mins close above VWAP. We can establish our buy level and our stop out level. The buy level was the high of the decision candle which is the candle that closed above VWAP and the stop out level was the low of the decision candle. So our buy level became $41. 37, and our stop out level was $41.27. So we waited for the next candle to open, and we waited for that price action to take place. Once the price action moved through the high of the decision candle, we initiated a long position with a 10 cents stop ($41.27). We can size our position size accordingly and we can let the trades start to work. As the price action started to move, we had a first point of consolidation which is the add opportunity. As you can see, the price action followed the blue line or the 9 EMA for the entire move and it never had a close below it until way up to the top. So once you are in the trade, you just need to follow the 9 EMA, and move your stop up until you get the first 5 minutes close below the 9 EMA

So with a 10 cents stop, this trade gave us over 1 dollar and 20 cents profit potential. That's over 10:1 reward to risk ratio. This is what great about the VWAP pop because normal the stop is relatively small and the profit potential is relatively large.

$KSS

This is the great example of a very good VWAP pop. The best VWAP pop comes from a stock that has a very hard down move initially. You can see, in the morning, this stock had a hard downward move and it started to pop up off the bottom which formed a nice looking V bottom. V bottom can give us the most potential of a VWAP pop. As the price action came from the bottom, it first cleared through 9 EMA, and VWAP and closed above VWAP. The buy level is the high of the decision candle which is $ 45.12, and the stop level is the low of that candle which is $44.89. This was a 23 cents stop. We got long at $45.12. As the move began to happen, it held above 9 EMA for the rest of the time until you got the first close below the 9 EMA where we can reduce our position. At that point, we received $1.16 profits from our entry which is 5 to 1 reward to risk ratio. As the price action continued to consolidate, it began to hold the 20 EMA. Since we were so far in the driver's seat, we want to try to hold on to this because it was holding the 20 EMA, and as the price began to move higher into the close of the market, we sold near the close for almost 1.6 points. Overall, it's a 7 to 1 reward to risk trade.

VWAP crack: the price comes off the highs, down through the VWAP and continues on down to the lows.

Setup

A stock in play must put in a lower high and/or rejected a key resistance level; preferably on the daily chart.

Allow a 5 minute candle to close below the VWAP and then wait for a retest of VWAP and a close back below; normally signified by an up-thrust, pin bar, or spinning top candles.

Initiating a position

Begin to initiate a short position as the price action confirms rejection of VWAP and moves downward away from the pivot candle. The pivot is the candle we just talked about which is normally in the form of an up-thrust, pin bar, or spinning top candles.

Determine your position size based on your risk utilizing the (1) pivot candle, and/or (2) the VWAP as your stop out level.

As the price action moves lower you may add to your position while trailing with a stop that keeps risk the same while increasing size.

Predetermine buy targets

Your first buy target should be the next clearest point of support, or, at least at a point that meets 2:1 reward/ risk ratio.

Always refer to the daily chart for the upcoming support levels and watch price action closely for further indications of direction.

Use the 9 EMA and a 5 minute close above as your indicator for further reduction of your position. As long as your price action stays below the 9 EMA, there's no reason for you to exit your entire position.

Trail the balance of position using lower highs/pivot points

$URI

Advantages

Easy to understand
The very first advantage of options is that the concept is easy to understand and you can start investing in it at the earliest. You can go through the meaning and concepts again to understand it better. Many youngsters find it easy to start trading in options and prefer it to the other types of stock market investments.

Flexibility
Options, as you know, allow you to remain flexible. You can either buy the option or refuse to do so. You have enough time to think about the deal and can walk away from it if you think the deal is not a good idea. This flexibility is what appeals to many investors as they have the chance to prevent their hands from getting burnt. You can also extend the time in some cases if you wish to conduct some more research on the topic.

Low Risk
There is a sense of low risk that is attached to options. This is mainly because you have the chance to know if or not a particular deal will work for you. You have to take time out to study the deal and see if it is lucrative. Only then should you go ahead with it. The risk factor will always count when you are investing a lot of money into it and dealing with it on a daily basis.

High Returns

The options market has the capacity to leave you with big returns. You will be able to control a lot of money with just a small investment. There are stories of how people have made thousands of dollars with just a small investment. How much you invest in it is completely up to you. But even with a small initial investment you will be able to gain a lot from your options.

Many options

As you know, there are many underlying securities in the options markets. You can look for particular securities to invest in like say just stocks or just foreign investments. The choice is yours and you can choose something that will work best for you. But remember to diversify it and choose different options.

Disadvantages

Risk

As you know, there are certain risks associated with trading in options. You have to exercise precaution and must not go all out at investing in a big way. The more precaution that you practice, the better it is for you. Try to understand everything that there is to about options first and only then should you invest with it. The risks involved will intensify because it is day trading. You have to remain alert and do as is right for you.

Low liquidity

You have to understand that options will have low liquidity. This means that they cannot be easily sold in the market. If you offer any of the underlying securities to the people in the market, then they might be a little apprehensive and find it tough to buy it from you. Even if it is a good security, they might still have their doubts about it. You have to sell it to them in such a way that they are convinced of its actual value. That can pose a challenge. The risk of illiquidity is what chases away many but if you understand how to sell options then you will not find it difficult.

Time lapse

One danger is that the options might take a little too much time to change in value. Maybe they will rise in value just a day after you refuse them owing to a fall in their prices. It is a little hard to predict the direction that these securities will take. You have to indulge in understanding the different prediction techniques if you wish to know whether or not the securities will do well. If you find it tough to do so then you can take the help of a friend who is well versed in it. Don't make the mistake of getting into something that you don't know works or not. Even if you do, tell yourself that it is a learning curve.

Information

There can be some spurious information out there, which might throw you off and confuse you. If you are receiving any emails from sources that you cannot identify then it is best that you not entertain them at all. Turn a blind eye to it and continue with your trading. Many rookies make the mistake of believing what they see on the Internet, news or emails. They assume that they are reading what is good information and end up making investment mistakes. You surely don't want that happening to you, especially if you are just starting out.

Not for all securities

Remember that options market is not open to all types of securities. There are only certain types like stocks, etfs etc. So, if you are looking for something very specific then you might not find it in the options market. However, that is a good thing for some as the options reduce and you will not have to go through a lot of details to find the best one for yourself. Many times, people make the mistake of having a lot of options and then choose the wrong one. That will be successfully eliminated if you wish to trade with options.

These form the different advantages and disadvantages of options. You can go through them once more if you wish to understand it better.

Chapter 6 Trading Strategies

There are a variety of different strategies which you can employ to ensure you make a good return on your day trades. Each of these strategies can be used independently or they can be mixed and matched, depending upon your overall personal strategy:

- Trend Following

As the name suggests your investment strategy focuses on the trends for certain share prices. This technique does not concern itself with whether the company is doing well or not; it is only interested in the trend of its share prices.

A trend is not a definitive guide to a successful trade, it is impossible to exactly predict how the market will react to any given news. However, a trend is a sign that something is doing well in the economy; regardless of whether it should be or not.

Sometimes the reason for the trend is obvious, such as a change in the foreign policy of a company or an increased threat of war. The trend should be obvious on a chart which shows stock prices and encourage you to look further. An upward trend could be nearing the end of its upward cycle; for this reason, it is essential to be cautious when buying the stock.

Ideally you should purchase some stock and watch the price; in the meantime you must calculate at what price you need to sell to minimise any losses. This approach can bring significant yields but it must be carefully monitored to ensure you do not find yourself dramatically out of profit. Indeed, if the price appears to peak, you should sell as soon as you are certain that the price is heading down again.

- Contrarian Investing

In essence this approach requires you to go against the current market trend; it is also the investment style of many of the investing 'greats', such as Warren Buffett and David Dreman; although many investors include this is their investment strategies. Of course, there is more to it than simply buying when everyone else is selling!

Day trading in this style involves looking at the 'hot' stocks; any shares which are rising rapidly and being chased by investors. This chase will inevitably push the price of these shares up into the buying fever is finished. At this point those who bought last will want to sell their shares before they lose extensively on their investment. This will trigger a downward adjustment and the share price will return to an acceptable norm. It is possible to buy and sell on the trend and hopefully make some profit. However, if you happen to buy at the top of the trend you are more likely to make a loss.

Whilst investors are chasing this big prize it is highly likely that they are selling shares in companies which are perfectly good but not offering much in the way of returns yet. It is these companies that a contrarian will be interested in. Shares in these firms have become undervalued as people chase the next big thing and they can be bought for a fraction of what they are worth.

These shares can be kept for the long term in the hope that they increase in value, or, they can be sold as soon as the market settles and a profit can be made on them. In effect, a contrarian investor is looking for the next big prize, before anyone else notices it. This can necessitate a long term approach if you wish to make the biggest gains. However, it can also be a very successful day trading approach as the market will always rebalance after a large amount of attention forces the price of one particular share upwards.

As the share price drops and people sell to minimise their losses, they will look to purchase the next rising star at a cheap rate; this is where you can make a sizeable return on any investment.

Perhaps the real beauty of this approach is that you have plenty of time to research the various companies; most other people are ignoring them. You will be able to locate the ones which are most likely to become the next best thing and invest as the interest develops; ensuring a healthy profit in one day!

- Range Trading

Many stocks trade within a specified range for the majority of the time. It is relatively easy to locate a range; simply look at a graph for the share prices for any given company over a period of several months. It will probably show several ups and downs. You will be able to draw a line through the peaks and the troughs. You must be careful to draw the line through the average highs and lows, whilst ignoring any particularly high or low one –off incidents.

Having established a range you will be able to monitor the stock and wait for it to dip below the range again. This will be the best time to buy the stock and sell it again when it returns into the range. Your established range should also give you an indication of how long it will take to rise in the range; you do not want to hold the stock for long to make your profit.

It is also perfectly acceptable to purchase anywhere in the range as long as the price of your stock is about to rise, according to your trend analyst. If your range shows a regular dip and rise you should be able to make a small profit regularly by simply following the trend. However, you should always act with caution as other market factors can alter the usual trend.

- Scalping

This technique can be very effective although you will require a reasonable amount of capital. It also requires a high level of discipline. The idea is to purchase shares which are at their asking price, or even just below; you then need to decide a strict policy of how much gain you are looking for. Many traders are happy with just one or two percent. As soon as the price rises to this rate, which is usually quickly as it is a small difference to the buying price, you need to sell the shares.

You will need to place between ten and two hundred trades a day, each trade will yield a small return but many small returns add up to a sizeable sum. The key to this strategy being successful is to pick shares which are at their bid price and to use your head, not your emotions. Your exit price must be adhered to regardless of what the share price is doing.

It is also possible to practice scalping by buying at the bid price and selling at the ask price; even if the share price does not move. The small difference between these two amounts can yield significant profits if you have both a large number of shares and are repeating the process many times with different shares. The only thing you need for this strategy to work is a buyer prepared to pay the market price; the shares are usually bought and sold in a matter of minutes.

- Rebate Trading

This is an extension of the scalping principle; in fact the two techniques are often used hand in hand. The difference between the bid and ask prices is created by demand. Those who wish to have their shares instantly will pay the ask price; this includes the fees and transaction costs; people who are prepared to wait for ownership of the shares will not have to pay the transaction costs and fees; however, they will have to wait and queue to obtain their shares.

Every transaction completed on the stock market includes a commission fee which must be paid to the ECN (Electronic Communication Network), this system is essential to allow people to trade from outside the stock exchange and allow individuals to operate on the stock exchange. However, this commission charge is not applied to the market makers, these are the people and companies who move thousands of shares a day by buying at the ask price and selling at the bid price. In effect these traders create the market spread which facilitates the movement of shares in the market. As a result of this they receive commission from the ECN instead of paying it.

If you can position yourself to receive commission, and gain profits via scalping, you can make a comfortable return on your investments with very little risk. You will need to choose a broker which specialises in ECN to ensure you can claim your commission.

- News Playing

Every year there are certain key reports published; such as the Non-Farm Payrolls report. These reports can have a huge impact in the stock market, however, there is no way of knowing what the report contains before it is realised and whether to buy or sell shares to maximise your profit.

Despite this there are many traders who will trade based on what they believe the report will say. Of course, if you get it wrong you can wipe out all your equity in one go! The higher the risk the greater the potential gains. There are several techniques to ensure you get the most out of these reports:

1. The slingshot is where you already have shares in the market and are waiting for the market to move in your favour; as soon as it does you will be in a great position to sell and make money from those desperate to join the bandwagon. The trick is then to be able to sell while the share prices are near their peak; unfortunately, it is impossible to know where their peak is.

2. It is also possible to identify the resistance points in the market; the low and high points relating to a particular share price. If the share price drops out of the recognised range while waiting for a specific report then it is a good indication that it is time to buy the shares. The report may be disastrous for share prices and push them down further; in which case you will need to know when to cut your losses. Alternatively the price can rise and allow you to make a reasonable profit.

The most important thing to remember when news playing is that the real gains are to be made when the market does not act as expected. A good bit of news will drive many people to purchase shares, expecting the price to rocket. When this does not happen, these people will panic and sell their shares. You need to be the person buying their shares while they panic, this will ensure you buy them low. Every time the market does not react as expected there is an opportunity to make money.

- Price Action

If you choose to use price action as your trading strategy, it means that you will always trade in the direction of recent price movements. This is an obvious technique if the price is steadily climbing; buy shares and sell them a little later in the day at a higher price. However it is often a little more complicated than that!

The price action strategy uses price and disregards any other indicators. This strategy is based upon the belief that a pure price chart shows you all the information you need to know, including all trades and the prices they traded at.

Deciding which shares to buy and when to sell is still a result of the statistics you can see, it is still possible to create a resistance area and the normal price range. The main difference is that the price is the only thing which guides you to make a decision on whether to buy or sell. Always invest according to the price action of the market, improving highs and lows indicate a market going upward and an opportunity to purchase shares, which can be quickly sold on for a profit.

- Candlestick Patterns

The Candlestick is a way of technically analysing the stock market and then using this information to decide which shares should be bought and when they should be sold. In essence the strategy is attempting to work out how other traders see a given share and what they are likely to do as a result of their opinion which will affect the price of the shares.

The candlestick is a way of viewing the data from a day concerning the starting and ending (or opening and closing) price of a given share. The information is displayed on a candlestick graph which shows the low and high for the share for the day as well. At a glance you will be able to see if your shares were up or down for the day. It is even possible to do the candlestick for longer periods of time.

This approach can alert you to when a market is about to collapse. In most day trading strategies you purchase and then watch the closing value. As long as it is higher than your buying price you are happy. However, it can plummet suddenly and leave you selling for a loss, scratching your head. The candlestick technique, which can even be used on an hour by hour basis for fast moving stock, will have shown you the beginning and ending price for each period. You will be able to see when the price starts to fall; even if it remains above the price you paid. This will allow you to make the decision to sell before it goes below your purchase price.

- Artificial Intelligence

Artificial intelligence is slowly becoming a part of everyday life. More importantly, it is being accepted as such. Computers are designed to crunch numbers and see patterns which are simply not possible to the human eye and this intelligence can now be used to study the stock market. As this technology develops the programs will have artificial intelligence and will be able to analyse the markets by themselves and locate the best places to invest to make guaranteed returns. It will no longer be a calculated risk but a certainty.

However, this may not become reality as there are many variables which can come into play through human behavior which can simply not be accounted for by an artificial intelligence.

In the meantime, there are a variety of algorithms available which profess to improve your chances of beating the markets. Whilst many of these systems appear to work it is not always clear why they do. It is an approach which may be worth considering depending upon your intentions.

Chapter 7 Money Related Financial Markets

Investors don't just put money in tangible goods; they also put money into "money" in the form of cash investment products. These markets include:

- Capital Market (handles both stocks and bonds)
- Bond Market (bonds are debt instruments similar to loans)
- Money Market

Capital Markets

"Capital" refers to the money businesses and economies need to operate. A company or individual can be very wealthy, yet still be very "cash poor." In other words, the company many hold valuable assets, but those assets are difficult to quickly turn into cash. Some examples include land, buildings, factories, mines, operating rights, and patent rights for a few examples. These are known as "illiquid" assets. "Liquid" assets on the other hand, include money in company checking accounts, and investment accounts, bank funds from lines of credit, and any actual cash the company has on hand. Businesses try to manage their liquid assets carefully. If they're holding too much capital in liquid form, their money is working for them. If they're not holding enough, they end up defaulting on loans or not being able to pay suppliers or workers. Growing businesses, as you read earlier, also frequently need capital to continue their expansion. While an individual who wants to raise cash most likely would go to a bank or finance company, businesses have more options for raising capital. It's the capital markets that provide these options.

Generally, the term "capital" markets refers to ways business can raise money either through the sale of equities (stocks through initial public offerings) or financial instruments such as bonds. One important difference between capital markets and "money" markets is the time frame of the transactions. money markets work with instruments of a year's duration or less, while capital markets are concerned with longer-term instruments. Another difference is that money markets work things such as U.S. Treasury instruments, deposits, and loans;

while capital markets deal with equities (stocks) and debt securities (bonds and debentures).

Bond Market

Bonds and debentures are forms of debt securities. One way a business can raise cash is by issuing a debt security. This is basically a loan from an investor rather than a bank. If company assets back this debt, it's called a "bond," if not, it's known as a "debenture." Obviously, debentures are riskier than bonds, since there is no specific asset backing them. These instruments are usually medium to long-term investments. The company will offer them at a discount rate it feels is competitive enough to attract investors, while being as favorable for the company as possible. Some factors that can influence the interest rate on the bond include its length to maturity, the financial rating of the company issuing the bond, and whether or not company assets back the bond.

There are ratings companies such as Standard & Poors, Moody's, and Fitch, which rate the safety of bond offerings. The higher the rating, the safer the bond is considered (if the company files for bankruptcy, bond holders have a higher priority on its assets than stock holders, but there's still a good chance they won't get all their money back). Bonds fall into several different categories based on their ratings. Generally, an AAA or Aaa (different ratings companies use slightly different designations) is the highest rated bond.

Bonds with rankings of BB+ to D (Baa1 to C) are commonly referred to as "Junk" bonds. Junk bonds will offer higher interest rates than investment grade bonds, since they are riskier investments. There's no sense for an investor to purchase a junk bond offering 3% interest if they can get a treasury bond paying the same rate.

As a day trader though, it isn't the bond interest rate or maturity that you'll care about. It's the money movements these things can affect. Bond can be bought when issued, and then sold by the original buyer, bought by someone else, then resold again. The question the buyer and seller share in the course of this transaction is "What is the bond worth?" Suppose the original bond was a $10,000, 10-year long-term investment that paid 6% interest. It's now two years later, and the bondholder wants to raise some cash. While the bond will pay back the original $10,000 when it reaches maturity, the buyer and seller must also consider how much interest that money will earn during the remaining eight years. The value of the bond can fluctuate greatly over the course of its life. Several things can affect the value of a bond. Let's take a look:

- Interest rate differences – Since it's possible to calculate the value of a bond over its life including interest distributions; it's also possible to compare two bonds value to decide which might be a better investment. In other words, if an investor has a choice between two $10,000, 10-year AAA rated bonds, each with eight years remaining to maturity and one pays 6% interest annually, while the other pays 5% annually, obviously, the first bond is the better value. If the owner of the second bond wants to sell his bond, then he needs to increase the value of his bond's sale somehow. This is done by "discounting" the bond value. The seller of the second bond will ask a lower amount for the price of his bond to make up for the lower interest rate. Discounted bonds are priced to account for this.

- Interest changes – in this instance, the value of a bond fluctuates as interest rates change. If you have a $10,000 bond paying 6% interest annually, with 8 years left of its 10-year maturity and interest rates rise higher than 6%, the value of your bond declines. On the other hand, if interest rates drop below 6%, your bond becomes more valuable.

• Company's financial rating – suppose you hold a AAA rated bond and all of a sudden, the company's credit rating drops to AA? The value of your bond decreases on the secondary market because it is not as safe an investment. The opposite is also true. If the company's credit rating improves, the value of your bond increases on the secondary market.

• Remaining time to maturity – the closer the time to the bond's maturity expiring, the lower the secondary market value will be since the bond won't be earning interest for very long.

• Market/investor confidence – the bond market undergoes swings in confidence just as the stock market does. During times of rising interest rates, bonds lose value, because bonds with lower rates and now worth less. If interest rates decline, then existing bonds paying higher rates are more valuable. This effect can be more pronounced if investors believe the interest rise or decline is part of an ongoing trend rather than a one-time aberration. It is this "speculation" that provides opportunities for the day trader.

The bond market offers the day trader some interesting opportunities. It generally (but not always) runs counter to the direction the stock market is moving. This is because investors tend to pursue better investments. If the stock market is rising, they invest more in stocks. If it is declining, then bonds and their greater safety, become more attractive, providing interest rates are reasonably stable.

Money Market

This market only deals with cash instruments with maturities of a year or less, since these investments are far less volatile than long-term bonds. During their short lifespan, they will experience fewer and smaller interest rate movements, the likelihood of originator default or downgrading is less, and, when investors stagger their purchases over a period of time, provide much greater protection from interest rate swings.

The money market is made up of "safe" investments. Typical examples of money market securities include short-term U.S. Treasury instruments, and highest rate municipal offerings and corporate "paper" (unsecured promissory notes of less than 270 days duration from highly rated companies).

Money market investments are usually purchased directly from the originator and usually offer much higher entry costs than other markets (i.e. your initial investment will have to be much larger than other investments because these securities are sold in much larger increments).

Money Market mutual funds provide access to this market for the small investor. They are useful places to park cash for the short term. Their interest rates tend to be low, so they're not good long term buys.

Chapter 8 Cultivate a Forex Mindset

When you are first starting out, it can be easy to feel as though the market itself, or perhaps the system that you are using, that is holding you back. Unfortunately, the truth of the matter is that there are other people who are in your same situation that are finding success, so there must be something more to it. That special sauce is a proper forex trading mindset and it is what separates successful forex traders from those who give up after the first six months.

The way you are wired

A successful trading mindset is actually a combination of three equally important things, the way your brain is wired, your mindset and psychological conditioning.

The way the brain works is that neurons fire in reaction to external stimuli and then travel along the easiest path possible to get where they are going. The more commonly used a path is, the more likely it is going to be used in the future.

These pathways then lead to habits and thoughts that form the basis for the things you do most frequently. When you put your pants on, do you always lead with your right foot? This is because the neural pathway that says this is the way things should be is much more worn in than the path that would see you lead with your left foot.

Furthermore, when the same group of neurons fires at the same time on a regular basis, the brain starts associating their various stimuli together as well. The end result of this is that thoughts that are unrelated on the surface can actually have major effects on the way your mind approaches the idea of trading. Generally speaking, the brain has three main functions, the first of which is regulation which handles all of the core physiological processes that keep you alive and kicking. The next is learning, which takes care of things like building new neural pathways and forming mental circuits. Finally, selection works with the other two to determine if the experience you are currently living through is worth storing away as experience for later.

All three are crucial when it comes to trading successfully in the forex market.

Regulation: Understanding how to keep your breathing in line as a means of relaxation is crucial to your long-term success as a forex trader. Learning to breathe slowly and deeply, and essentially forcing yourself to relax, will help to prevent you from feeling emotional, panicked or stressed when trading, improving your overall successful trade percentage in the process. Failing to do so means you are going to be more likely to miss crucial details or make decisions that you would not make if you were in your right mind. Luckily, this is an easy skill to improve upon and you can do so by practicing yoga or mindfulness meditation.

Learning: The easiest ways to accelerate the learning process is to spend more time considering the feedback the market gives you, practicing your system or training with a mentor. Once you get into the habit of making learning a lifelong goal, you will find that you naturally improve as a forex trainer.

Selection: In addition to learning, taking more time to experience what the market has to offer will provide you with additional feedback and context that will help you naturally learn what strategies and practices are naturally more valuable and beneficial to your personal trading style. This will occur naturally as you discover what practices tend to make your money more consistently compared to those that do not.

Hardwired for survival: While modern society means you have had to learn countless bits of information that would be completely useless out of context, you have also picked up a wide variety of survival strategies along the way, likely many more than you might expect. These may not all be well-adapted for use in everyday life, however, which is why it is important to learn about why you think about certain things in the way you do.

For example, when the brain takes note of a high energy signal it typically triggers an alarm response which naturally triggers a host of nonproductive ways. Survival strategies to be aware of include:

- Prioritizing stability during periods of constant change

- Creating cause and effects relationships

- Attempting to avoid pain while seeking out pleasure

Depending on your trading style, prioritizing stability can either be a useful tool or one you will want to work to change. If you have a low tolerance for risk, then you will want to go with the flow and seek out stable trades when the market is in flux. However, if you prefer higher risks and greater rewards then you will want to be aware of this instinct so that you can more easily ignore it.

When it comes to being on the lookout for cause and effect scenarios, it is important to always keep in mind that the human mind is naturally fond of patterns which means that it likes to find them even in places where they might not actually be. As such, when you come across what you believe to be a relationship it is important to take a closer look and ensure that it really exists before acting on it in a way that you may regret later.

If you find yourself seeking to avoid pain and seek out pleasure, you are going to want to do what you can to change this mindset as soon as possible. Risk and reward are intertwined to the point where you cannot get one without the other. If you brain associates risk with pain, then you are going to need to do whatever it takes to change that mindset ASAP. Regardless, understanding why you may feel uneasy about a given trade, even after doing the necessary research will make it easier for you to push forward, eventually rewiring your neural pathways in the process.

Maximize your beliefs

Take a closer look at your beliefs

As a new trader, the sheer potential awaiting you in the forex market must make the possibilities seem endless. However, after you hit your first serious obstacle, whether that's a serious loss, misreading the market in a major way or any one of dozens of common new trader issues, you may find that your enthusiasm for the process overall may weaken. This, in turn, can make it even more difficult to trade successfully while at the same time dragging the goals you have set for yourself even further out of reach. If left unchecked, this can be the start of a pattern that can make it difficult, if not impossible, to be as successful as you would like.

These types of thoughts are known as limiting beliefs and they can manifest in a wide variety of unproductive trading habits. These include things like forcing yourself to overextend in an effort to double up after a previous loss, using more leverage than is prudent, variating from your trading plan without a good reason for doing so or doubting yourself when it comes to making a completely viable trade. Likewise, if you find yourself hesitating when it comes to determining a viable entry or exit point or making excuses for trades that ended up not working out in your favor, including blaming the market, then you might be dealing with limiting beliefs.

These beliefs may have already been a part of your subconscious, or they may have been created as you learned the wrong lessons from early trading experiences. The source of these issues isn't nearly as important as the fact that they are limiting your ability to trade successfully, and they need to be culled from your trading habits if you hope to turn a profit in the long-term. Whether you are aware of the fact or not, the market is essentially a mirror that affects what is in your mind. It doesn't have any actual biases, it simply reflects back your beliefs about yourself and your trading skill.

As such, when you engage in limiting beliefs, you are letting them deceive you and costing yourself money in the process. On the contrary, engaging in healthy, energetic, vibrant and clear energies will allow you to focus on the best your mind has to offer, improving the percentage of your successful trades as a result.

Moving beyond your limiting beliefs: The two most important traits you need to strengthen your mindset and banish your limiting beliefs are awareness and recognition. To start, you are going to want to make every effort to build up your awareness in such a way that it can be applied directly to your trading experiences. Doing so will allow you to see the way in which your limiting beliefs are directly tied to your successful trade percentage. It is this level of recognition that is required before you can realize not only that you have been unsuccessful but why exactly it is that success is eluding you.

You may find it useful to think of trading in the same way you would riding a horse. Specifically, it is bumpy and can often leave you feeling as though you are not in control. However, if you do your best to stay in the saddle, then eventually you will have enough knowledge to apply what you have learned so that you can progress on your way to success. Applying concentration and awareness to your daily training routine will help you build up mental strength and confidence as you see it lead to greater and greater success. This, in turn, will lead to an increase in trading skills from reading price action to being more disciplined.

Improve your posture: While not something you would likely expect to affect your mindset; the truth of the matter is that your physical posture can go a long way towards destroying any limiting thoughts that might be lying about. Specifically, you are going to want to ensure that you are sitting straight, with your spine properly aligned. This posture will improve not just your thought process but the way you breathe as well.

Keeping your spine straight will make it easier for your energy to move from your head directly to your heart, which will, in turn, allow you to think more clearly. If you sit with your neck bent at an odd angle, it limits the flow of this energy and isolates your head from this natural flow. If you often feel as though you are stuck in your head, this could very well be the reason why.

Improve your focus: In order to improve your focus during the trading day, you will want to start off with a round of mindfulness meditation to improve your ability to focus and make quick decisions in the moment. To begin, you simply try and remaining as fully in the current moment as possible by breathing slowly and taking the time to really listen to everything your senses are telling you. Start by slowly breathing in and out and focus on every second that this action requires.

From there, the biggest hurdle you will have to face is learning how to dismiss your thoughts without interacting with them. Mindfulness meditation is all about existing in the present as much as possible and listening to everything your senses have to tell you. In order for this to be the case, you must make a concentrated effort to keep your mind as clear as possible. No one's mind is ever truly free from other thoughts and ideas, however, which is why it is important for you to make every attempt to reduce excess thoughts as much as possible.

To do this, you must first make it a point to not feel angry or sadden at the fact that your mind is not completely clear, feeling something in relation to the thoughts is akin to interacting with them, the last thing you want to do. Instead, it may help to think of your mind as a blank space with bubbles floating through it. When a stray thought appears in a bubble, simply visualize it floating away and popping, removing the thought from your notice. Once mastered, this same technique can be used to ensure you maintain self-discipline and focus on the task at hand regardless of whatever it may be.

Become more aware of your positive thoughts: If you feel yourself starting to lend unreasonable credence to negative thoughts, you may instead find it useful to counter this influx of negative with an influx of positivity instead. Doing so will allow you to more clearly see the instances where your negative thoughts are trying to influence your actions, leading to a more stable trading experience as a result. With practice, this will also make it easier for you to improve your understanding of the market and improve your confidence as a result.

While the positive energy generated by this practice will likely start off as a slow trickle, if you nurture it you will find that it becomes a raging river before you know it. This will, in turn, make it easier for you to avoid engaging in excuses, negative emotions or anything else that is sure to have a negative effect on your ability to trade effectively.

Chapter 9 Strategies for Day Trading Beginners

To those people who are not yet fully knowledgeable on the field of day trading, they have to take note that it is a dangerous endeavor. People can lose a lot of money if they make hasty trading decisions without any solid understanding of the concepts.

Entry Strategies

Not all investment assets are profitable for day trading. A day trader searches for volatility and liquidity in equities. Liquidity allows him to trade a security at a food price. Volatility, on the other hand, is the range the daily asset price can move. If the asset is more volatile, it means the day trader can either make a great profit or suffer a significant loss.

A day trader can use Intraday Candlestick Charts, Level II quotes/ECN, and real-time news service to determine the possible entry points for trading. The candles offer analysis of the price movement of the security while the level II quotes and ECN offer a preview of the orders as they occur. Lastly, the real-time news service updates the day trader as soon as the news comes out.

There are candlestick patterns that a day trader can use to search for a possible entry point. One of the most reliable patterns is the doji reversal pattern.

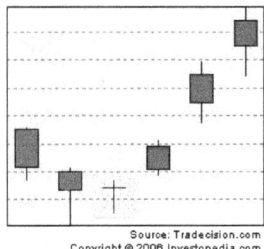

Source: Tradecision.com
Copyright © 2006 Investopedia.com

Looking at candlesticks - the highlighted doji signals a reversal.

A trader searches for a doji reversal pattern with different confirmations. He needs to search for a volume spike to confirm if there are traders who support the asset price at that level. Next, he needs to look at the previous low-of-day or high-of-day price level. Lastly, he checks the Level II situation to determine every open order and size. By following these steps, he can find out if the doji will reverse its position so that he can enter a position.

Popular Day Trading Strategies

Scalping
Scalping involves purchasing then selling the security as soon as it becomes profitable. Upon breaching the price target, the day trader sells his security immediately.

Fading
Fading allows a day trader to short a security after the price goes up rapidly. It assumes that the security is overbought, the current buyers are scared to buy and the early buyers can begin locking in their profits. Fading is risky but extremely rewarding. A day trader's price target is that price when the buyers start buying the security again.

Daily Pivots
Daily Pivots is a strategy, which profits from the daily volatility of the security. The day trader attempts to purchase the security at the low-of-day and sell it at the high-of-day price. The price target is the price at which the security shows a possibility of reversal using the doji reversal pattern.

Momentum
Momentum is a strategy used by a day trader to trade a security based on news release. Sometimes, he also searches for strong trending movements with high volume. He buys the security then rides the

trend until it begins to show a sign of reversal. The target price is that price wherein the volume starts to decline and bearish candles begin to appear.

The entry strategies used in day trading are similar to normal trading. However, a day trader normally exits the position when there is decreased interest as shown by the trading volume and Level II/ECN.

Using Stop-Loss

A day trader who trades on margin must use stop-losses to limit the losses on a particular position. He can either use a physical or mental stop-loss order. He puts a physical stop-loss at a particular price level, which matches his level or risk tolerance. In essence, it is the price that the day trader can afford to lose.

He also places a mental stop-loss at the price, which violates his entry criteria. He immediately sells his security when the trade does not go as expected. In addition, he sets a maximum amount that he can lose in a single trading day. Once the total daily loss reaches this amount, he closes his positions and rests for the day.

How to Evaluate Trading Performance

Majority of day traders lose their hard-earned money. However, a day trader with a well-defined strategy can improve his probability of success. He has to follow his chosen trading strategy, instead of monitoring his gains or losses. By doing so, he can identify potential problems easily and finds solutions for them.

Chapter 10 Using Technical Analysis

When it comes to ensuring that your successful trade percentage only increases as time goes on, you may find it useful to branch out of analyzing the fundamentals of a company to determine if its stock is worth considering and to also analyze it technically. Technical analysis studies past market trends with the goal of accurately predicting those that are likely to occur again in the future. Technical analysis is ideal for those that like the idea of determining future performance by looking at previous prices, without having to dig through mountains of paperwork to find the details you are looking for. While the past will never be able to truly predict the future 100 percent of the time, technical analysis is useful when combined with a basic understanding of market mentality for generating predictions that are accurate within reason.

Price charts: A price chart is a core part of technical analysis; essentially, it is a chart with both an x and a y axis where the price can be seen along the vertical axis and the time can be seen along the horizontal axis. While there are plenty of different charts to choose from, each with their own unique strengths and weaknesses, those that you will want to keep in mind early on include the line chart, the candlestick chart, the bar chart and the point and click chart.

Line chart: The line chart is the simplest of all the charts because all it does is show the closing price of a given stock over a set period of time. The lines, in this case, are formed once the grouping of closing prices has been determined and then connected with the end goal of showing a trend. You won't be able to find details such as what the opening price for the same period of time was or what the overall results for the day were but you will be able to determine if the day over day is positive which is still quite important which is why this is one of the first charts that day traders of all skill levels consult when they are looking into the details of a new stock.

Bar chart: A bar chart expounds upon the details provided by a line chart by providing a greater degree of detail regarding the specifics of the day. The top and bottom of the bar represent the high and the low for the day respectively while the price at closing is indicated on the ride side of the bar with the help of a handy dash. The dash on the left side of the bar shows the starting price. and if the stock increased in value for the day then the bar will be black while it will either be red or clear if the price decreased throughout the day.

Candlestick chart: A candlestick chart is similar to a bar chart, though the information it provides is much more detailed overall. Like a bar chart it includes a line to indicate the range for the day, however, when you are looking at a candlestick chart you will notice a wide bar near the vertical line which indicates the degree of difference the price saw throughout the day. If the price that the stock is trading at increases overall for the day, then the candlestick will often be clear while if the price has decreased then the candlestick is going to be read.

Point and figure chart: While seen less frequently than some of the other types of charts, a point and figure chart has been around for nearly a century and can still be useful in certain situations today. This chart can accurately reflect the way price is going to move, though it won't indicate timing or volume. It can be thought of as a pure indicator of price with the excessive noise surrounding the market muted, ensuring nothing is skewed.

A point and figure chart is noticeable because it is made up of Xs and Os rather than lines and points. The Xs will indicate points where positive trends occurred while the Os will indicate periods of downward movement. You will also notice numbers and letters listed along the bottom of the chart which correspond to months as well as dates. This type of chart will also make it clear how much the price is going to have to move in order for an X to become an O or an O to become an X.

Trend or range: When it comes to using technical analysis successfully, you will want to determine early on if you are more interested in trading based on the trends you find or on the range. While they are both properties related to price, these two concepts are very different in practice which means you will want to choose one to emphasize over the other. If you decide to trade according to trend, then you are more interested in going with the flow and choosing stocks to trade while everyone else is having the same idea.

Your goal in this instance is to then determine what trends are going to manifesting themselves in the future so that you have as much time to take full advantage of them as possible. If you are interested in trying this type of trading you will want to make smaller than average trades as it can be risky as you never know when a trend will fail to materialize in the way you might have previously hope it would. Trading via trend is a good choice for those who prefer high risk and high reward trades.

If you are interested in a safer trading strategy, then you will want to consider range trading instead. When you are trading on the range, you are instead looking for stocks that you can reliably predict with relative confidence will make a positive movement before moving back to about where they started from before repeating the cycle once more. You don't need to find the perfect entry point in this instance, you simply need to get in at a point where you will be in on the ground floor the next time the cycle repeats itself. Range trading can take more time to get working properly, however, so it is best to have a larger bankroll when aiming to successfully put it into effect.

Chapter 11 Favorite Intraday Charts and Patterns

There are HUNDREDS of chart set ups out there that people claim to be working for themselves and that is absolutely fine. We all know that there is NO winning chart set up that works all the time. If anybody tries to sell you something that is guaranteed to make money in the stock market, you know it's BS. You just have to find what works for yourself and more importantly, stick to it. Whenever I trade, I always look for a few patterns which I'm most familiar with and trade them, I discard everything else which I don't understand. In this chapter, I will share the 3 top patterns I look for to go both long and short respectively.

Remember, you don't need to be following hundreds of different kind of set ups to be successful, streamline your process and focus on those with the highest probability of success.

Long Setups

1) Bearish Open on Bullish Daily

This is my *favorite* type of long setup because I have had the most successful trading it.

What you are looking for in this type of chart is that it must have a large audience following the daily chart. This could also work on a bearish daily chart but I always find that this works better on the bullish daily chart, which means the stock has been going up steadily for a few days. In the morning, you want to see a very weak open, which means the chart has opened lower than the close of the previous day or if the stock has plummeted at the opening bell. This is normal in a bullish chart because many people want to take profits in the morning especially when the chart has been gradually trending up and they get a little shaky in their emotion. If this set up occurs, you will want to watch this stock carefully for an entry.

If the stock plummets at the open and people are taking profits, we want to be waiting until a higher low point happens to get long. NOTE: Some stocks reverse sharply and bounce straight up without doing a double bottom. Chase these stocks at your own risk if you believe that there is a good risk vs reward. I'm usually conservative and wait for a higher low to form before placing my entry. This is a classic chart and as I've said, my favorite type of longs because it is easy to follow and gives me a very clean and favorable risk versus reward. In this type of long, you typically want to place your risk on the low of days. Once the chart fails to hold its higher low, take it off and reassess the chart! Never let the chart take you for a ride and you will never bust your account.

OPK - The stock dips at about 9:40am at the open. Notice that it starts forming a higher low point between 9:45am and 9:50am. We want to enter at $14.20s with risk based on $14.15.

GPRO - GPRO plummets sharply at the open. Higher lows starts to form between 9:45am to 9:50am. I will buy long at $42.25 and risk the low of day at $41.75.

2) Multiple Time Frame breakouts from consolidation

It is a breakout over the line of resistance that is across a longer time period, usually 3 to 6 months. It is important that the support and resistance lines are growing tighter and tighter at the breakout so that more people are anticipating it. It should be at the tip of a triangle shape at the point where it is about to breakout. The more people that are anticipating it, the stronger the breakout will be. They will want to jump on the wagon once the breakout happens and not wanting miss the trend. If you are trying to find these types of charts, you can simply head over to finviz.com and filter the charts by "horizontal line of support/resistance". The site gives you a nice list of charts that may fit into this category.

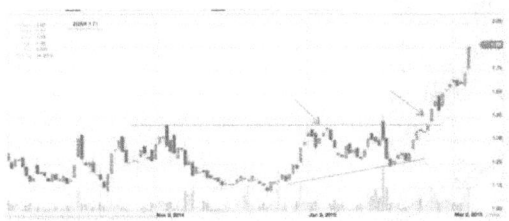

ZGNX – The daily chart breaks out at $1.50. It has been testing the highs for about 3 months. We want to buy the break out at $1.50 and anticipate a good push.

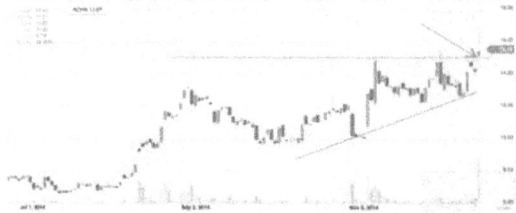

ACHN – Daily chart consolidated at around $14.90 for a couple of months. Notice the sharp increase in volume when the chart finally breaks $15.00. We want to get a long position when the breakout happens and take advantage of the spike.

3) Perk and Go on Bullish Daily

This long set up has excellent potential of spiking HARD. If you can couple this with the MTF breakout setup mentioned above, it will give you the most value for your bucks. If this set up pops up on the stock on my watchlist, I will definitely go long, provided that there is a good risk versus reward. However, it is not always easy to find these charts and they are rare to come by. Generally in this type of charts, you are looking for a bullish daily chart. In the intraday chart, you want it to be slowly perking up towards the high of day. The key to identifying this is to find a bullish chart that spiked up at the market open and slowly slide back down due to profit taking. After this period of profit taking and the stock price forms a bottom, the chart slowly starts to perk back towards the high of day. This is where you want to get long with a risk based on the bottom of the dip.

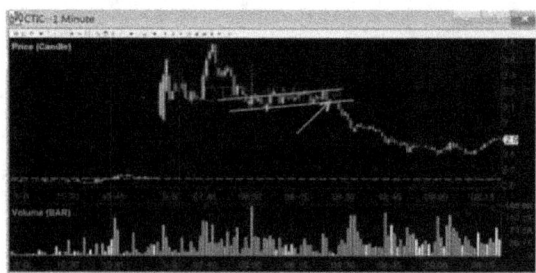

Chapter 12 Using Candlestick Charts as Part of Your Strategy

Understanding the entry strategies that you can use will help you to figure out how to navigate the market once your overall market strategy has been configured. Additionally, it's important to note that"strategy"here means how an investor figures out what he or she is going to purchase next. The craziness of the stock market is mostly due to the fact that nobody truly knows for certain what is going to happen next. For this reason, multiple strategies on how to day trade have been developed. They all work sometimes, and then all fail at other times. That is the nature of the market. Your job is to pick out which strategies appeal to you the most, and then use then as much or as little as you'd like.

What the Heck is a Candlestick Charts

A candlestick chart is a chart that's used in the stock market to gauge how money is moving throughout the day. The picture below of a candlestick chart should be able to provide you with a better explanation of how it works.

Can you see from the picture how the candlestick chart received its name? As you can see from the example above, the color of the candlesticks reveal whether or not the stock is in the red or in the green, respectively. The tip of the candle, where the candle would be burning if it were actually a candle and not a chart, indicates the highest price point for that stock on a given day. If you look at the green candle, the "Close" indicator there tells you where the price was at when the stock market opened. It should be obvious that a green-colored candle indicates that this stock closed higher than its opening price, and it's colored red if the stock closed lower than its opening price. If you look to the bottom of the green candle, you should be able to see that the "Open" arrow is pointing to the spot where the stock opened at the beginning of the day. The "Low" portion of the candle below the word "Open" is able to show you the price when the stock was at its lowest price throughout the day. The only difference between the red and green candlesticks that are shown above is that the opening and closing prices are at opposite ends of the graph. One other difference that you might see in some of the candlesticks charts at which you look is the fact that they are usually either filled in with black or left open.

As is evident, this candlestick is not filled in with a green or red color; instead, it's filled in with black, meaning that the closing price at which the stock is set was lower than the price on which it opened. On the other hand, when the candlestick is not filled in at all, this means that the stock closed at a higher price than which it opened. One other factor that is important when seeking to understand the candlestick chart is that the length of the actual body of the candlestick can also help you to figure out how well a stock is doing. For example, when the length of the candlestick is long, this means that the market is going through a "bearish" period. When the stock market is bearish, this means that for one reason or another a lot of pessimism exists in the market. Maybe a particular economic decision has just been passed or a new government official is taking over and is causing a lot of widespread doubt. These are the types of reasons why a market would be bearish, and this results in a mass selling of stock.

Contrastingly, if a market is particularly bullish, this is basically the opposite of a bearish market. For whatever reason, no one is selling their stocks, and this can create a situation where stocks are priced higher than usual. Instead of being black, these lines will appear as long and white. This make sense. If no one is selling their stock, the price of the stocks would appear stagnant, and you'd end up with higher overall prices. When it's a bearish market and people want to get out fast, it's likely that the price of the stock will drop due to the desperate nature of the stock market. When it's a bearish market, investors are more likely to feel like the stocks are going to plummet, and they'll want to get out while they can. For reasons such as this, they'll be more likely to drop their selling prices in exchange for an overall feeling of security. The picture below can help to better illustrate to you the concepts of bullish and bearish markets.

The Shadows of a Candlestick Chart

One other aspect of the candlestick chart is what's known as the "shadow". We have already discussed the shadows briefly. They are the wicks of the candles that protrude from either end of its body. These too, just like the body of the candle, can differ in size. When the shadow is short and is paired with a body that is filled in with black, this means that when the stock market opened, this share was closer to its highest point for the day than when the day was done. When the shadow is short and the body of the candle is white or gray, this means that when the stock closed it was near its high for the day. As you can see from the chart above, the candlesticks on the candlestick chart can vary greater from one another in size, shape, color, and length.

The Notion of a Spinning Top

You can see the phrase "spinning top" etched into the chart that's found above. A spinning top is added to a chart when the difference between the amount of times the stock has been traded between the open and close price is somewhat neutral. These can be found to be either black or white, depending on the preferences of the person or group who creates the chart, and are typically much smaller than most of the lines that exist on the chart.

Doji Lines

The last type of structure that exists on the graph about which we'll discuss is known as the doji line. This type of line can also be seen on the graph that is located above. The doji line can show the investor periods of time when the opening and closing prices for a particular stock were almost exactly the same. This is the smallest figure that will exist on the graph, with the spinning top being the second smallest element.

After learning about the ins and outs of candlestick chart, it should be fairly easy to see how you can start using this tool for your overall strategic goals. The candlestick chart is used by thousands of day traders and even other types of investors so that they can keep track of the closing and opening prices for a stock in which they're interested. If you think back to the concept of a reversal, it is fairly easy to pinpoint on a candlestick chart when a stock might be taking a turn for the better or for the worse.

Chapter 13 Bollinger Band Strategies

Bollinger Bands can be used to trade in the forex market successfully because they are an effective signal when it comes to markets being overbought or oversold. As the most profitable currency discrepancies tend to work best when currencies are in one of these extremes as part of a trend.

The default Bollinger band setting is based on the 20-day moving average and has two standard deviations. The upper band is typically 2 standard deviations above the 20-day moving average and the lower band is set 2 standard deviations below the 20-day moving average. The underlying asset then trades between these two prices with oversold levels reaching the lower band and overbought levels toughing the upper band. The band's width then represents the volatility of the underlying asset.

Basic trading strategy: In general, assuming that the market is in an uptrend, you will want to use the overbought readings of the Bollinger band to purchase currencies depending on the strength of your convictions that the trend will continue as well as your overall aversion to risk. If the price hits the higher of the two bands then you will want to take some profits from the expectation of a revision of mean or through the digestion of the overbought conditions.

Bollinger band strategies tend to be the most effective in markets that are currently trendless. Under these market conditions, oversold and overbought readings are always going to be more potent. This is due to the fact that competing forces are currently pulling the market in both directions.

It is also important to keep in mind that price has a strong preference towards fluctuation when it comes to the central band. You will need to be able to detect this fact reliably if you want to successfully make use of any of the strategies outlined below. You will also need to be aware that the top band acts as resistance while the bottom one acts as support. In order to find the best results when it comes to using the Bollinger bands, you will want to display them on charts that are at an hourly range or higher as the additional information will make it easier to parse what is really going on.

All about trend

In order to truly use Bollinger Bands effectively, it is crucial that you understand trend and how it factors into the effective analysis. A trend can be in any direction on the chart, as long as it indicates the direction the market is likely to head in next. Trends can be either obvious because of how strong they are or practically invisible because they are weak which means it is important to not discount a pattern from the start just because it isn't all that strong quite yet. This is not to say you should go jumping at shadows, however, as the human brain is fond of latching onto what it thinks are patterns that are little more than random configurations of data.

As you might expect, this is easier said than done as the price is rarely going to move in a single direction for long. Rather, it is going to move in clumps of lows and highs if a true trend is forming. This means that you can often get away with just focusing on those highs and lows as all that you are going to see in the middle is meaningless static anyway. This doesn't mean that you should only look for lows and highs that are grouped together, however, as what you should really be looking for is a pattern of higher highs, in stark contrast to what came before. Additionally, if you are following a negative trend then you are going to want to be on the lookout for a pattern of lower lows for the same reason.

An uptrend is a positive trend while a negative trend is a reversal; you may also run across horizontal trends where all of the highs and lows balance out into nothing much of interest to anyone. You will also want to keep an eye on the length of the trend you are following which can either relate to a short-term trend and intermediate trend or a long-term trend. The longer the amount of time the trend has lasted in the past, the greater the amount of time you can confidently expect it to last when it comes around again.

Shorter trends can actually be part of trends that are much longer overall, which is why it is important to always double check and ensure you aren't making a move on something that is only an offshoot of a much larger, and much different trend. To make the process of deciding what's what even easier, it is important to always keep an eye on the weekly, daily and yearly charts if you want to locate any truly long-term trends. If you are looking to get rich quick, however, then you will want to stick to the daily charts instead.

After you have found an especially interesting trend, the next step is going to be drawing a trendline which is as simple as drawing a straight line that correctly illustrates the direction the trend is currently moving in. When it comes to an uptrend, you will want to draw your line in such a way that it connects the dots of all of the lows in such a way that the line is below the relevant data. If you are looking at a reversal trend then you are going to want to draw the line so that it connects the highs, leaving the data below the trendline.

This line can be seen as the resistance level of the market which is the maximum amount of movement it is likely to experience the next time it does move. The one thing this line will not tell you is the odds that this next move is going to be positive or negative, just what the amount is likely going to be.

You will also want to keep an eye out for channel lines which are a pair of lines to the side of the data you are watching that indicate the levels of resistance and support that are in play. One trendline connects the highs while the other connects the lows while the resulting channel can either go up or down, or even sideways, but the interpretation will always remain constant. The goal should be to establish a channel that is long enough to show a break from the data that it has been following. This breakout point will mark the best time to get in on the trend you are following to ensure that you have the maximum amount of time to profit from the trend you have discovered.

Choose a tool to follow trends: While it is possible for especially savvy traders to make money when it comes to trading against the trend of the market, it is much easier for most traders to just go with the flow and trade on the trend. This is easier said than done, however, if you don't utilize some type of method for adequately pinpointing trends as early on in the process as possible to ensure that the potential for profit off of every trend that is successfully found is as great as possible.

While some people will swear that a trend following tool is really all you need to get started trading successfully, in reality, they are only really helpful when it comes to helping you to determine if the right choice in the current market is to enter into a long position or if a short position is a better choice. One of the easiest, and as a result most reliable, trend measuring tools to use is what is generally referred to as the moving average crossover.

- *Crossover: A crossover is a point on a chart where the currency you are tracking and the indicator that tells you when to buy or sell intersect. Taking this a step further, a moving average crossover is a way to determine an upcoming change in the trend of a price related to the currency in question. A moving average is a technical indicator which is used as a means to more easily smooth out the otherwise somewhat disparate movement of the price of a given currency. It is considered a lagging indicator as it can only ever function as a reminder of previous prices.*
- *Simple moving average: Unlike a traditional moving average, a simple moving average adds in a bit of arithmetic by calculating the price of the given currency over several different time periods and then dividing that total by the number of time periods that are taken into account in the process. When using this process, it is common for a successful trader to keep an eye out for averages in the short term to cross a point that is higher than the current average in the longer term which is a common signal for an uptrend.*

Bollinger band strategies to try

60-minute Bollinger band strategy: This strategy uses a pair of Bollinger bands as well as a momentum indicator. The timeframe for this strategy is going to be 15 minutes, with an expiration time of 60 minutes which should give you four full candles to work with. The Bollinger bands will have the standard 20-day EMA with the pair of bands each sporting a standard deviation of 2. You will then want to ensure the momentum indicator is set for 11 periods.

If you are looking to purchase a call option in this scenario then you will want the price of the underlying asset to be above the middle band at the very least. Furthermore, the momentum indicator should be north of 100 as well. When it comes to puts, you are going to want to purchase a put option only if the price is below the middle band with a momentum indicator that is lower than 100.

For this strategy to be effective, you will need to ensure that both of the conditions for the type of option you are considering are met before you determine your entry point. If there is a cross in the middle Bollinger band but the momentum indicator is still less than 100 you will want to avoid making calls. The same goes for puts if the momentum indicator is higher than 100.

Scalping Bollinger Bands: This strategy is useful when dealing with underlying assets that are a part of the forex market, specifically the GBP/JPY pair, commonly known as the Dragon. This name was earned due to the extreme movement the pair often sees in a single day with ranges of between 100 and 200 pips being the average. Luckily, this strategy makes the pair far easier to tame than would otherwise be the case. Even still, you will only want to use this strategy if you have a very high tolerance for risk and once you have a firm grasp on the basics of options trading.

This system revolves around an Exponential Moving Average along with a pair of Bollinger bands and is useful with virtually all currency pairs and time frames. With that being said, the most common and effective timeframe tends to be 5 minutes. Bollinger bands are a type of technical indicator which defaults to twenty periods with a standard deviation of two. However, with this strategy, you want to set one band to twenty-one periods with a standard deviation of two and the other to twenty-one periods and a standard deviation of three.

The end goal here is to locate periods when the price touches a point that is between the pair of standard deviations. Once this occurs you will want to use a moving average of 200 as the guideline that allows you to accurately monitor the trend. If the price rises above the 200 point, then you can profit from long positions and if it drops then you can profit from short positions. At the same time, you will want to keep an eye out for a candle to form and close inside the space between the two deviations. If the opposite occurs then it indicates a reversal.

When the conditions outlined above are met, then you know that you can open a trade at the start of the next candle with minimal risk. You will want to place a stop-loss either above or below the candles depending on the type of trade you are making. You may also want to set the target at the average of the pair of Bollinger bands with a second target set at either the upper or lower line, depending on the type of trade you are considering. This system has proven effective in virtually all situations as long as you take into account the price as it relates to the moving average of 200. This is a somewhat complicated strategy to put into practice so making a few low-impact trades with it is recommended before moving to the big time.

Chapter 14 Establishing Yourself as a Trader

Trading stocks as your sole business could help anyone gain lifestyle and financial independence. Trading will provide you flexibility in your lifestyle and possible, unmatchable financial gains, but it also comes with many financial risks. If you are planning on becoming a full-time trader, you will have to establish yourself into the right mindset and the right resources. As with any business venture, you will need to take time for planning and preparation in order to succeed. Also, when you list yourself as a trader on your taxes, you will be able to take higher losses.

Here are some tips on how to get yourself established as a day trader:

- Pay off your debts as quickly as you can. The debt will sit over you and you will end up letting it influence your decision whenever you trade because you are trying to get a lot out of every transaction. If you push trades like this will lead to choices and transactions that don't follow your trading guidelines.

- Start a fund and give it its own bank account. As with any business, you might be strapped for money when you are beginning, but do whatever you are able to create a separate fund than your savings so that you can protect the financial security of your family.

- Come up with a trading strategy. This should include how you plan on picking the stocks you are going to buy, when you are going to sell, and when you are going to purchase them. If your write all of these things down, you be able to create a prescribed business system

- Read financial journals such as *Barron's* or *Wall Street Journal* and online resources regularly. These will provide you with a lot of daily information you are going to need about anything that will affect your investment including industry specific, economic data, and political developments.

- Open a discount trading account online. There are different online brokerage firms that provide you with different trading fees. Link this account to the one you opened for trading.

- Make a trading budget and limit the amount you invest in one stock. Your budgets should include weekly and daily limits for your trading.

- Make a spreadsheet that will track your investment. Create guidelines when you made purchases and sold stocks and everything that it cost. There is financial software that you can use to help you with this so that you are ready when tax season rolls around.

- Stick to your buying and selling strategies. Be very careful when it comes to your budget. Ups and downs will happen, never go away from your guidelines. Not having discipline will lead to bigger failures and losses.

- File IRS form 4797 with your taxes to get more than the standard investor's losses against your capital gains. Having the term trader is unclear to the IRS. Somebody that is a trader for a living and who seeks short-term gains should qualify. Find a tax adviser if you have questions about qualifies as a trader on your taxes.

The financial software will help you keep track of sales and purchases with security description. You will need this for IRS purposes. Keeping excellent records will avoid this problem.

Deduct your home office expenses against your business. You could deduct a part of your rent or mortgage, phone lines, internet access, and computer equipment. Tax advising, publication subscriptions, and software are all deductible.

Trading isn't for everyone. If you are thinking about full-time trading, start with a considerable amount of money to test your discipline and strategies before you launch it as your sole means of income.

Chapter 15 Handling Your Money

Even people who are really good at managing their money and sticking to a budget may struggle when it comes time to be able to manage the different aspects of the trading process. This, when it comes to day trading. You need to try different things that will help you to save your money, and that will prevent you from spending too much money while you are trading the different amounts of money that you have. It is important that you work to make sure that you can use each of these things to make your trading experience more enjoyable.

The different monetary contingencies that you can put into place are all different and are all intended to be able to help you save money while you are making money. You can choose to use one of them or use them all, but they will help you while you are working on becoming a day trader. Just make sure that you know what you are doing and that you are using them in the proper way. Many of these contingencies are created for people who choose to automatically trade the different things that they have while they are buying and selling stocks during the course of a day.

Limiting Trades

There are some things that you will need to limit to be able to get the most out of the day trading process. For example, you may need to limit the number of times that you trade a certain stock, the amount of money that you put into one stock or the way that you can trade different things. By putting limits on everything that you have, you will be able to ensure that you are going to get the most out of the process and that you are going to be able to enjoy the benefits that come along with trading while you are still managing to save a lot of money on the different processes and on the different price points that you have in different areas.

You can choose to make your decision based on a single trade – for example, you can limit the number of times that you have put the one trade up or you can choose to do it with multiple ones. There are many different combinations that you can make with the trading process, and it is important that you include everything that you need with each of the different options that you choose to put on your limits. Each limit may have a different approach.

When you are setting up the limits that you have on things, you will need to either decide that you are going to do it manually or automatically. Manually will require you to review the process on a daily basis to make sure that you are not going too far above your limits. With the automatic limit setting, you will have limits that will be set ahead of time and will apply to all of the different trades that you do on a daily basis. The choice is yours and will depend on the way that you do things.

Budgeting

Creating a budget for your stocks and your day trading options is nearly the same as creating a budget in any other aspect of life. You need to decide how much you can afford to spend and what you are going to make. With day trading, you also need to figure out how much you are going to put into the trades on a daily basis. This is the limit that you want to be able to stick to each time that you do different trades and on a daily basis. It is important that you work to make sure that you are creating a budget that is completely reasonable for what you want to spend and what you could make throughout the day. You should be sure that you are going to get the most out of it by setting a budget that is reasonable for you.

As long as you are modest with your budget and you plan for any incidentals that could go on with your trades, you should have no problems sticking to the budget. It can be hard to be able to stick to the budget in your personal life, but it should be easy to do it when you are trading different things. As long as you know the amount that you want to spend on a specific day, you should always have a good idea of what that is going to mean for your business and your different trading options. Doing this will allow you to enjoy all of the benefits of trading without having to deal with the problems that come with reckless spending on investments.

Targeting for Price

You should always have an idea of how much each of the investments that are present in your portfolio should cost. This will help you with buying as well as selling and will give you all of the help that you need when it comes to the different options that are included in your portfolio. It is important to make sure that you are going to be able to make money back. If you don't know what something is going to cost you, you may struggle to figure out how much money you are going to get back for it.

Set a target for the price of a stock that you are going to buy. To do this, you must learn how much you want to be able to buy it for. Find out the value of the stock, the amount that you can get for it later on when you *do* decide to sell it and the average amount that it is going for. Stay within that target price. No matter what happens with your pricing options, make sure that you try to stick to the target price that you originally set. It may be hard to be able to get everything that you need out of it but knowing what your target price is should be enough to help you.

It is also a good idea to set a target price when you are selling your stocks. By knowing the value (and tracking it), you will be able to know what you want to get for it. If you try to sell it at any point throughout the day and you aren't going to be able to get the most amount of money for it, simply try later on in the day. Just be sure that you are not waiting too long to be able to get the money from it because you may end up missing out on the sale that you can get from the stock and you could end up with having the stock stuck in your portfolio at the end of the day so that you are unable to start the day with a clean slate like you are supposed to while you are day trading.

Stop Losses

If you have a stock that is eating up too much money or that is pulling out money from the amount that you want to be able to get, you can always put a stop loss on it. This means that it automatically gets cut off after you have lost a certain amount of money on the stock and that you don't have to worry about it draining anymore of the money that you have in your account. A stop loss is useful for people who use automatic stock options and who want to make sure that they are going to be protected if something would happen that their money is being drained by stock.

A stop loss is a great contingency to have in place if you are planning on doing automatic trading. This is not always the case for people who are new, so it is not something that you will probably need when you are first getting started but just be sure that you know that it is available. Once you start to use auto trading, you should always have a stop loss in place to cut off once you have reached a certain amount that is being taken for the stocks that you wanted to buy originally.

Available for Loss

Everyone sometimes loses when it comes to trading. The real question comes in how much you can lose and what you can do to get the loss out of the way of your trading. The loss is something that you need to be careful with but is also something that you will want to deal with as it comes. It can be helpful to set an "available for loss" balance that you are comfortable with losing.

By knowing the amount that you are comfortable with losing, it will make losses less of a shock to you and can make it easier for you to want to be able to continue trading even after you have started to lose money on the trade. There are many different options that you can set for your loss balance but usually keeping a set amount of money in your balance available to trade is the easiest way to do that.

Always protect your money when you are trading. The point of trading is to make money, and if you are unable to do that, you may not be able to get the most out of the trading process. You should have a good idea of what you have, what you want to be able to have in the future and every other aspect of trading. There are many different options that people who are trading may have to select and to make the right choice is always going to benefit you. It is good to make money, but it is even better to make sure that you are protecting the money that you already have. Losing is difficult, but it can be hard to rebuild money that you had in the beginning.

Chapter 16 Ways to Manage Your Time as a Day Trader

This book has been chalk-full of techniques and strategies that you can use to grow your existing or aspiring day trading strategies, but we have yet to talk about day trading in a sense that goes beyond the strategies within day trading. Of course, everyone who participates in day trading has a life and it is extremely important that this life is not compromised because of the desire to win money. We have all heard horror stories of people who become obsessed with the stock market and end up throwing their children's tuition down the toilet. Don't let this happen to you!

Time Management Technique 1: Choose a Trading Strategy that Meshes with Your Personality and Lifestyle

One of the most important factors for any day trader is to choose a strategy that coincides rather than contrasts that individual's overall personality and character. For example, if you're the type of person who can be patient amidst chaos and you are able to naturally resist the urge to sell and purchase stock through fear or anxiety, then the truth of the matter is that the lifestyle of a traditional stock trader might work better for you than would the life of a day trader. If on the other hand, you find that you are constantly antsy and can't stop thinking about what you're going to do with your money next, then the life of a day trader is right up your ally. This example is certainly not to try and convince you that day trading isn't for you, but if you are somewhat laidback, then don't you think that day trading is going to cause you anxiety that you're not traditionally used to experiencing? Your trading strategy should coincide with your overall personality, and this requires that you know yourself well enough to choose a trading method that works well for you.

Time Management Technique 2: Take the Time to Look at Charts

Of course, there are areas of day trading that you might be able to skim over and still be successful, but ignoring charts and empirical information is not one of these factors. Even if you don't have much time on your hands, looking at and understanding a chart prior to investing in a stock is far more important than performing guesswork and hoping for the best. If there's anything that you should take from this book it's this: take the time to understand empirical data, and if you don't have the time then don't bother wasting your money on a trade.

Time Management Technique 3: Learn to Systematically Absorb Information

We have already discussed the fact that you can develop templates for yourself for when you're writing in your trade journal and conducting a post-trading analysis. Time management should be no different. Success often comes from the little things, the detailed information that is sought after and calculated day in and day out. Having a systematic and disciplined way of processing information will keep you working towards the same thing every day, and this creates predictability. Often, it's much easier to be successful when you have a process that works for you, rather than finding that you're all over the map.

Time Management Technique 4: Don't Try to Force Time

When I say, "Don't try to force time", what I really mean is that you should never try to force a deal if the conditions that you'd like to see simply aren't there. If you're always eager to trade constantly and quickly, you are going to make mistakes and these mistakes are ones that often could have been avoided if you had been more patient. To reiterate, many day traders are in disbelief when they hear that other successful day traders sometimes go days without making a trade, but this is the truth of the matter. You don't have to force trades if they just aren't there for you, and you don't have to make a trade every single day just because you're a "day" trader. If you're uncomfortable with the conditions of a certain trade, listen to your instincts. Even if it turns out that you're ultimately wrong and you find out that you should have traded after all, you'll at least be privy to this knowledge without having invested any money in it in order to find out.

Time Management Technique 5: Avoid Distractions

Of course, most investors want to be watching the news in the morning so that they can get a feeling for the climate of the market on a particular day, but often times the news eventually starts recycling itself and the television becomes more background noise than anything that's concretely useful. This type of background noise can quickly go from being helpful information to being an unnecessary distraction. It's important that you can delineate between the two. A good plan for yourself would be to set a time for when the television is on and when it's time to turn it off. Additionally, you can do the same thing for your phone. Have your phone on during certain hours of the day, and turn it off turn peak trading hours. This again requires discipline. Lastly, avoid the temptation to go down the rabbit-hole of watching YouTube videos or surfing Facebook. These tasks that you think will only take a minute end up taking entire hours of your time, and before you know it you're losing tons of money.

Time management may not seem like a necessary topic to cover when discussing the stock market, but for a day trader time management is often essential to overall success. This is particularly true when discussing the strategies of both the contrarian and momentum philosophy. If you have a family, time management and the stock market is essential. Even if you think that you could earn money during all times of the day, having a balance between when you should be trading and when you should be spending time with your loved ones if often essential to maintaining your sanity.

Chapter 17 Trading Psychology and Risk Management

Here are the three things that make day trading works: (a) trading psychology, (b) critical business methods, and (c) effective and efficient risk management strategy. It is a typical mistake for a beginner to focus exclusively on business indicators and strategies.

A good business strategy leads to positive expectations. It generates more profits than losses over a period of time. But remember, even the most careful strategy does not guarantee success in every operation. No strategy can assure you that you will never have a loss or even go through a series of exchange losses. For this reason, risk control should be an integral part of any commercial strategy.

The trader's inability to handle the money losses is the primary reason for their failure on daily trading operations. It is a common tendency for people to accept profits quickly and also wait until the levels of loss are balanced again. By the time some new traders learn to manage their risk, their accounts are bad, if not irreparably damaged.

To be a successful trader, you must learn the rules of risk management and then implement them firmly.

Learning the risk management strategy and firmly implementing it are the keys to succeed in trading. You need to set boundaries that will limit you to placing decisions. From time to time it will be necessary to admit losing and say: "I was wrong" or "The configuration is not over yet" or "I'm getting out of the way."

Risk Management In Three Steps

Step 1: Before you begin, identify first the maximum money you will place on trading. The money you are willing to risk should not be more than 2% of your bank account.

Step 2: From your entry, compute your maximum risk per share and strategy-stop loss in your chosen currency.

Step 3: To know the total number of shares you can exchange from time to time, divide it with the amount you get on step 1 on the amount you will get on step 2.

For instance, having an account of $50,000 will limit you to a transaction of $1000 according to the 2% rule. However, if you want your risk to be smaller, you can choose the 1% rule which will limit you to the amount of $500 per transaction.

They buy the shares at $20 and want to sell them at $23, with a difference of $18.50. You will risk only $2 per share. This is another way to control your risk.

To determine the size of your stock, you will divide $500 (your transaction limit) by $2 (which is your risk per share) which will get you an answer of 250. This means than you have 250 shares (the maximum shares you can buy and exchange).

From there, you will understand how stop loss is used based on technical analysis. Your trading plan will also depend on the size of your account which only you will be able to determine that.

The decisions will come from you definitely. For instance, if your stop is higher than your moving average, you need to compute if your stop is higher than your maximum account size at risk or not. If your stop in the moving average results in a $700 loss and has set your maximum loss of $500 per transaction, you need to temporarily pause from trading and patiently wait for another chance to trade.

You can argue that it will be difficult to calculate the stock size or stop the loss based on a maximum loss in your account while waiting to enter operation. You have to make a decision quickly. Otherwise, you will lose the opportunity. I understand that it is difficult to calculate the loss limit and the maximum loss of the size of your account in live operation.

Why Do Most Traders Fail?

Day trading is not supposed to be easy. Trading needs practice, and I strongly recommend that new traders paper trade under supervision for at least three months in a live simulated account. It sounds crazy at the beginning, but you will quickly learn how to manage your account and your risk per trade. You will be amazed at how rapidly the human brain can do calculations on what share size to take and where to set the stop loss.

Day trading requires self-discipline and ability to make immediate decisions. If you hear the latest news that an activist investor has just joined Amazon.com Inc., your first reaction might be to load the boot. I can hear the logic that forces you. "Let's buy 5,000 shares on Amazon! Let's make a big order!" But you need to be able to make a quick decision about whether to buy, sell or sell that inventory, and you need to make that call with discipline.

Your ability to maintain self-discipline and mental control will eventually lead your trading strategies to improve overtime. It's hard enough to know what the market will do, but if you do not know what you're going to do, the game is lost. The new commercial strategies, the tips you will get from me or this book or even the most sophisticated software I can imagine will not help the traders who cannot handle themselves.

Evaluate yourself with the following questions:

•   Is this strategy suitable to my trading approach?

•   If this my trading strategy won't work well, where will be my stop?

•   How much money should I risk on trading that will grant me a chance of winning?

This is what many traders find difficult. All of these decisions, the process that guarantees that these decisions are adjusted to their risk tolerance and strategy parameters, are misleading multitasking. Not only is it multitasking, but also multitasking under stress.

Chapter 18 Day Trading Tips

This chapter will include tips, rules and advice about day trading. They are not in any particular order, however, they are all important. It may be hard to see or understand their importance as you are just starting out, but over time and with experience, you will come to understand their importance.

A written Plan: If you are planning to trade without having a written trading plan, then you are going to find yourself all over the place. You will be wandering from strategy to strategy, from system to system and from market to market with no direction. You need to have a written trading plan to give yourself focus and accountability.

Trading simulator first: You will be saving yourself a lot of money by learning everything you can on your trading simulator before you do any live trading with real money. It is also a good idea use your simulator to test out new techniques before you apply them in the marketplace to make sure that they have positive expectancy.

Use an adequate account size: The minimum account size of a pattern day trader is $25,000. That's the absolute minimum. When you first start out, you will probably have some losses so you want to make sure that your balance will also cover that and also keep the balance above $25,000. If you are planning to trade stocks, the minimum account size is $50,000. Should your account be too small, you will have to consider other markets that don't require such a high balance. You can always move on to trading stocks later on after you start making money if that was your intention to begin with.

Stops: We've talked about stops a few times. Never ever trade without stops! If you are thinking that it would be ok to trade without them, then you aren't ready yet. And you should go on the simulator a bunch of times and see what happens when you don't use any stops. It will be a matter of time before you are facing a very big loss.

Setting initial Stops: Don't set your initial stops too wide. If you do, then you may not make enough profit to justify taking the risk on the trade. The risk to reward potential won't exist for a day trade.

Taking profits too soon: If you take your profits too soon you can actually lose money. I know it sounds crazy. However, most day traders are working with systems that just naturally may have less than 50% winners. And so that means that your winners must be at least a few times more than your initial stop so that you don't end up with a negative expectancy and lose money.

FOMC Fed Meeting Days: No trading. Just go have fun!

Do your Research: In order to maintain your confidence and keep investing your money in not just the market, but essentially in yourself, you need to do your research. It's very important to understand how the characteristics and statistics of strategies and systems before you use them or trade them. If you don't understand, you will completely bail out of the system or strategy the first time that you hit a losing streak or a drawdown. You must be familiar with the streak statistics of any system. You will have a much easier time of trading through a system's five consecutive losses if you have completely tested it and you understand that it's a common occurrence.

Market to Market: Starting out, it's not a good idea to move around from market to market. For example, don't move from stocks, to futures, to currency, etc. It can be a huge distraction and will prevent a new day trader from concentrating, learning all they can and excelling in one market.

Risk Management: If you want to be profitable, you must practice good money management. This falls in line with making a plan. A good trading strategy will allow you to have multiple loses without wiping out your trading account. However, the quickness with which those loses deplete will depend on what percentage you risk on each trade.

Treating it as a hobby: If you seriously want to make money at day trading, then you absolutely must treat is as a job and not a hobby. A hobby is collecting stamps or building models. You have to take the time to formulate a plan, learn, do your research, and decide what your goals are so that you can keep track of your progress.

Options Trading: Trading in options offers huge returns so for people who have a small amount of money to work with; this seems like a great idea. In fact, brokers actually require an additional application for this type of trading. On the other side of huge returns are huge losses. And someone has to be losing that money. It is a big mistake to get involved trading options until you have more experience. It is volatile and complicated and should be avoided until you have learned it well. If you listen to no other advice about where to begin trading, listen to this advice. Steer clear of options for now.

Leverage: We haven't really touched on leverage in this book, however, you are bound to see it mentioned. Leverage is equal to getting a second mortgage or using the title to your car as collateral. That's basically what it is. I don't believe it's wise to trade with leverage. And if you do your research and your homework and you formulate a good proven strategy that works well, you shouldn't even consider trading with leverage. Trading with borrowed money is extremely risky especially when trading such volatile stocks.

Risk – Reward Ratio: This is pretty simple. Try to keep your risk reward ratio at 3:1 so that you lose small and win big. Then your wins always make up for small losing streaks.

Conclusion

Congratulations! You have now completed one of the most comprehensive books about day trading for beginners. You should now feel ready to begin your new career as a day trader.

By now, you have gained more insight on day trading than you had when you picked up this book. Not only do you know what day trading is, but you know what a typical day is like for a trader. On top of this, you know a few bonus tips on how to manage your time, you know several common mistakes that day traders make (that you can now avoid), and you know the right mindset that you have to work towards in order to reach success as a trader.

Of course, you have also learned different day trading strategies and platforms that are commonly used. You have learned about the steps you need to take before you begin trading, such as creating your business or trading plan and all the research that goes into learning about the profession. You have also read about creating a watchlist, how important your trading plan is, and how to execute your trading plan when you begin your day trading journey.

This book also touched on a few stocks that many day traders look at throughout their day and factors that will help you in choosing the best stocks for you. Furthermore, you have learned that there are different types of brokers, how to find the best broker, and the rights you have when it comes to working with your chosen broker.

Although this is a comprehensive beginner's book, your research and learning journey as a day trader is not over. There are many other resources that you can look into, including the resources included in this book. I want to see you succeed in your day trading career and, therefore, I hope that you will take the information from this book with you as you begin your journey. Best wishes and happy trading!

Dividend investing:

Step by step Guide for beginners to start creating your way to financial freedom and a passive income and build your blueprint. Includes ideas and secrets made easy to build a passive income.

Description

In today's world, we all have a sense that we need to grow our money. Many people would also like a source of passive income and a way to add to their income in retirement. Living off Social Security isn't really an option for any quality-of-life. Unfortunately, far too many depend only on Social Security. It wasn't that long ago when people could rely on FDIC insured banks to not only grow their money but also to act as a source of passive income. Bonds, which are basically loans that a private individual makes either to a government entity or to a corporation, also used to be a reliable way to earn interest payments off your money. Back in the days when you could earn 6 to 10% interest from bonds, it was a very safe and lucrative way to earn money. It's hard to believe that in 1990, which really wasn't that long ago, you could buy US treasuries and earn solid money off them every six months. You also have the guarantee of safety for your principal that was in the hands of the United States government. Of course, today, the government is in massive debt and the debt continues to grow. Now, the government is threatened by rising interest rates. Already, paying interest is practically becoming as large a part of the budget as the defense budget is. Can you imagine a world in which the government is paying more money for interest on its debt than it is for national security? That is a pretty crazy situation.

So, as we alluded to in the introduction, there is still a safe way that investors can protect their principal at least to a certain degree and earn a passive income. This is by investing in dividend stocks.

There are different ways that you could do this, but one way that provides the remarkable benefits of growth that the stock market can provide, with at least a certain degree of safety, is to invest in solid companies with growing dividend payments. Later in the chapter, we are going to look at a few companies that serve as examples. But before we get into that, let's explain what dividends are and how they work for people who are beginners when it comes to the subject of dividend investing.

This guide will focus on the following:

- Basic overview
- How to pick dividends
- Buying dividend growth stocks for retirement
- Analyzing dividend stocks
- Dividend yield
- The REITs
- Minimum reasonable expectation
- Why do companies paying a growing dividend have excellent stock market performance?
- Key elements that define insider and outsider group membership
- Dividend growth stock suggestions to start your portfolio
- How pick a technically and fundamentally stock for dividend portfolio
- Having the compound interest force on your side!
- Tip checklist for the new EFT investor... AND MORE!!!

Introduction to Dividend Investment
What is Dividend Investment?

Dividends are referred to as the distribution of after-tax earnings of a company to shareholders in relation to the number of shares they hold. Mind you, there are 3 parts to this definition, and each one is equally important. Firstly, dividends are paid from profit and not from any other source of equity, for instance, paid-in surplus. Secondly, dividends must be in the form of real assets, and this part is quite tricky. It is a common habit for companies to pay out dividends in the form of cash, checks, or more stocks, since these are convenient. However, it would be quite difficult and nonsensical for an airline company like Boeing to offer the right wing of a 747 to a major shareholder as dividends. Nevertheless, during high levels of inflation, we have seen corporations pay dividends in the form of products that they sell. Finally, the third part of this definition states that every shareholder has a share in dividends irrespective of the number of shares that they hold in the company.

So, How Did It All Start?

You might wonder: how did companies start paying dividends and who started the whole concept? Well, dividend-paying stocks have been around for hundreds of years, and it has provided an infallible source of passive income to investors for many generations. Here's the outline of the history of dividend-paying stocks.

1250

A French bank called Société des Moulins du Bazile was the first company to pay out dividends.

1602

Nearly 400 years later, the Dutch East India Company became the second corporation in history to pay out dividends. Over the course of its 200-year existence, this company paid out 18 percent of its capital.

1682

Dividend investment finally officially came to North America. The Hudson Bay Company is arguably the first to pay dividends; the first dividends were paid about 14 years after the inception of the company in 1670and were worth half of the stock value.

1910

In the early 20th century, many investors were only interested in stocks paying dividends. During this period, stocks were expected to have higher dividend yields than bonds in order to compensate investors for the risks that come with most equities.

2003

After 28 years of growth, tech giant Microsoft declares its first dividend payment.

Today, about 420 companies out of the 500 company stocks on the S&P 500 pay a dividend. This includes giant corporations like Chevron, McDonalds, and Wal-Mart.

Terms to Know in Dividend Investment

Before we proceed into the countless benefits of dividend investments as a passive income, here are a few terms you first need to get familiar with. These terms will not help you to breach the world of dividends but will enable you to make better financial decisions during investments.

Cash Dividends

Cash dividends are cash payments made to shareholders as part of the company's accumulated earnings or current profit. This is a way for the company to return profits to investors for the shares they hold. Companies pay out dividends monthly, quarterly or yearly. Besides normal dividend payouts, shareholders can also receive special cash dividends after legal settlements or a one-time cash distribution.

Declaration Date

This is the date on which the board of directors in a corporation announces the next dividend payment. Also referred to as the announcement date, the board of directors announces the ex-dividend date, the dividend size, and the payment date.

Dividend Cover Ratio

The Dividend Cover Ratio is the ratio between a company's net dividend to shareholders and its earnings. This is an analytical tool used by investors to gauge if a company's earnings can sufficiently cover its dividends to investors. You can calculate this by dividing the earnings per share by the dividends per share.

Dividend Reinvestment Plan (DRIP)

This is a plan offered to investors by dividend-paying corporations to re-invest their cash dividends. The DRIP is an amazing strategy that you will come across in the course of this book. By re-investing your cash dividends into more shares, you will earn higher dividend payouts. Furthermore, most Dividend Reinvestment Plans allow investors to buy additional shares at a discount and without commission, however, most Drip don't allow a reinvestment that's less than $10. If your company doesn't offer a DRIP, you can set one up with a major brokerage firm.

Dividend Yield

Dividend yield is a term you need to add to your repertoire. It is a financial ratio that, in relation to its share value, depicts the amount a company pays out in dividend each year. You can measure the dividend yield by dividing the yearly dividend per share by the share price. This term represents the total amount of return from an investment, and it's the perfect tool to measure potential investments.

Here's how to calculate a dividend yield. Let's assume Company ABC is trading at $40 per share and the company offers a yearly dividend of $1.5 per share. Therefore, the dividend yield would be at 3.75%. You may have noticed that the share price and dividend yield move in the opposite direction. If we selected a higher share price of $60, for example, the dividend yield would decrease (1.48 dividend ÷ $60 per share equals to 2.45% yield). Therefore, you can earn more dividend income if the share price is lower.

Record Date

Companies determine their shareholders on the record date.

Ex-dividend Date

The ex-dividend date is one of the four main important dates to dividend investors. This is the fixed duration on or after which a security is traded without a formerly announced distribution or dividend. Additionally, it is also the date on which the seller of a stock will be entitled to a recently declared dividend.

Payment Date

This is the date on which a stock dividend is scheduled to be paid to shareholders. You should know that only those who bought their shares before the ex-dividend date can receive dividends on the payment date.

One-time Dividends

Also referred to as special dividends, these payments are larger than the conventional dividends paid out to shareholders.

Rules of Dividend Investments

Dividend investments, just like any other niche, comes with its own set of rules. Think of these rules as short-cuts to avoid making common mistakes. These rules are backed by academic research and principles from some of the world's greatest investors. Mind you, don't think of these rules as infallible since there will be always be an exception. Nevertheless, it's good to integrate these rules into your everyday investment decisions.

Always Go for Quality!

Long-term orientation is one of the best advantages an investor could ever have. It is a rule to invest in businesses that have stability, profit, and a proven track record showing growth. Why should you go for a mediocre business when you can invest in a high-quality business? As a financial rule, you should rank stocks by both their dividend and corporate history length, and the longer they are, the better.

The Bargain Principle

It is a rule to invest in businesses that pay you the most dividends for the cash you invest. Remember, the higher the dividend yield, the better. In addition to this, avoid investing in overpriced securities. You should only deal with stocks trading below a decade historical average valuation multiple, which is the average value of stocks calculated over a ten-year period.

Always Play Safe

Avoid businesses that pay out all their income as dividends, as this means that the business has no margin of safety, and dividends can be reduced at any time.

Reinvest Your Dividends

This is one rule you must never break. The power of reinvesting your dividends cannot be undermined. In fact, putting your dividends back to work can do wonders for your portfolio. What's more? You can make use of reinvestment programs, which often enable you to reinvest your payouts automatically without paying a commission fee.

Understand Your Tax Laws

Warren Buffet once said that he is taxed less than his secretary. So, how does he do it? Well, most of his income comes from dividends, which are indeed often taxed, though lower than standard income. So, get familiar with the tax structure for dividends and take note of any changes resulting from new company or government policies.

Don't Make Dividends Your Only Priority

Dividends are an indispensable part of investing. However, dividends are not the all-mighty metric to abide by. Investors need to pay attention to different fundamentals that are often at play in investments. Fundamentals like profits, price actions, and earning growths are just a few of the features you need to pay attention to. Remember to look beyond high dividend yields and ensure you understand the company's growth pattern and prospects.

Watch Out for Value Traps

Many investors jump at seemingly lucrative stocks without realizing that they are value traps. A value trap is a phenomenon where a dividend yield is increasing, and stock prices are reducing. When faced with this phenomenon, most investors think they've hit the jackpot. However, they fail to realize that the stock prices were reducing for a legitimate reason. So, how can you detect this trap before it is too late? Here's the first sign to watch out for. When you see a company that pays out far more than its peers in the sector or market index, this indicates a value trap. In addition to this, falling cash flows with stable yields also indicate a value trap.

Always Look Out for Special Dividends

One of the perks of dividend investments is the ability of corporations to initiate a one-time dividend payout. When looking for stocks to purchase, these one-time dividend payouts often mislead investors. During one-time dividend payments, a company's stock might seem rosier than normal. A good example is Microsoft (MSFT), who issued a one-time dividend payment in 2004 which was a sharp contrast to the normal dividend payouts. Microsoft's normal dividend payouts varied from $0.3 to $0.5, while the one-time dividend payout was a whopping $3 per share. Many resources calculate the one-time dividend payment as an annual yield. If we were to include the special dividend payout, Microsoft's annual yield for 2004 would have been 13.78%, instead of the 0.38% payout from normal dividends. As you can see, the figure was enough to confuse investors who hadn't checked and analyzed the yield statistics.

Use the Survival of the Fittest Principle

Sell your stocks when your dividend payouts are reduced or cut short - it's that simple. Research carried out between 1972 and 2017 showed that stocks that cut or reduced their dividend payouts had a 0% percent recovery. If your dividends are reduced or stopped, this obviously goes against the principles of generating passive income. In fact, it is the opposite of what we are aiming for. Any business that cuts its dividends has lost its competitive advantage. Therefore, you want to reinvest the proceeds of your sale into a more profitable stock.

How to Manage Risks in Dividend Investing

Like any form of investment, there is always a risk in stock dividend investing. But the risk is always variable and unpredictable. Some factors can increase the risk of this type of investment. Some of these factors are within your control, while some are not.

While it is impossible to completely get rid of the risk, it is still possible to minimize our risk exposure. You can do this by understanding the factors that play behind the sentiment in the stock market.

Savvy investors are skilled in managing risks in stock dividend investing. They are trained in dealing with factors that are within their control.

Human Error

Human error is the biggest risk factor in stock dividend investing, which could lead to the following:

- The disconnect between investment goals and investment strategy

- Allowing emotions to control your decision to buy specific stocks

- Giving in to fear and panic in making decisions

- Lack of research and analysis

- Negligence to monitor market conditions

In order to prevent human error, the best way you can do is performing due diligence.

Let's say you need to jump out of a building during a fire. What would you feel if you are not prepared for such a situation? You will certainly feel extreme fear and you will experience panic that could even worsen your situation.

This is like stock dividend investing. What would you feel if you believe that the stock market is crashing? You might panic and decide to cash out all your holdings because you are afraid to lose all your money.

Diversify

Never put all your eggs in one basket. This is a piece of classic investment advice, and it is timeless because it is true.

Stay away from the idea of investing all your money in just one company or one industry. You never know what will happen tomorrow, so don't bet all your cash on one player.

As a mere shareholder, you may not have any voting rights or administrative privileges to direct the company. So, you don't have any control over the business management.

Moreover, the company or even the entire industry may go against the investor sentiment. All of these are beyond your control.

One of the few things that you can control is the investment instruments where you pour your money. You can significantly minimize the risk by distributing your investments in various dividend stocks.

We'll explore the importance of diversifying your dividend investments in

How Will You Receive Your Dividend Payouts?

For cash dividends, you will usually receive the payout in the form of a check or electronic bank transfer.

For stock dividends, you will usually receive the payout as stock options. You will not receive any check, but just a notice about the increase in your additional shares. You may choose to cash out your shares or retain it if you think the share price will continue to increase.

Investors who are receiving cash dividends are often sent a check after the former dividend date or the date when the stock starts trading without the declared dividend.

Meanwhile, some companies release extra shares that are equivalent to the value of the dividend payout. This method is called dividend reinvestment and usually offered as an option for dividend payment by individual private companies or mutual funds.

Remember, dividend payouts are taxable income regardless of the method that you have received them.

Some companies have Dividend Reinvestment Plans or DRIPS. If you are interested, just add your existing equity holdings with any added funds from dividend payouts. DRIPs can make the process easier compared to receiving the payout in cash and then using it to buy additional shares.

In-house DRIPs are usually free from agency commissions because there is no need to pay for brokerage fees. This feature makes it attractive for beginners as commissions are proportionately bigger for smaller share purchases.

Another benefit of joining a DRIP is that some companies are providing stockholders a choice to purchase more shares in cash at a much lower rate. The price discount can be as high as 10%, aside from the additional benefits of waived brokerage fees.

Hence, you can purchase more shares at a lower price compared to stock investors who purchase stocks in cash via brokers.

When Do Companies Release Dividend Payouts?

Companies who decide to issue dividend payouts will notify their shareholders usually via a formal press release. And for easier reference, the announcement will also be documented through major stock quoting services.

After the announcement, the record date will be determined. The record date refers to the specific date that the shareholders will receive the payout. One day after the record date is known as the ex-date. This refers to the specific date that the stock begins trading at "ex-dividend".

You are not qualified for the dividend payout if you buy shares on an ex-date. The payable date is usually 30 days after the record date. During the payable date, the company will transfer the value of the dividends with the Depository Trust Company (DTC).

The DTC will then distribute the dividends to the different brokerage agencies where shareholders are holding their stocks of the company.

After receiving the payouts, the brokerage agencies will deposit the dividends to individual client accounts.

If the investor is enrolled in a DRIP, the brokerage will start processing the reinvestment plan in accordance with the instruction of the stockholders.

Holders of preferred stocks are often given priority for claiming the earnings and assets of the company. These include the claims for dividends. So preferred stockholders will be paid first, then the rest will be distributed to the owners of common shares.

- **Basic Overview**

So, first things first. Right now, the stock market continues to provide a way that you can grow your money at a pace that is faster than inflation. Many people are understandably leery of the stock market because they lived through at least the 2008 financial crisis, and many others are old enough to remember both the recession after the 9/11 terrorist attacks and the dot com recession that happened in the late 1990s. You also don't have to be that old to remember black Tuesday in 1987. So many people have a misperception of the stock market-based in part on those crashes and based on the misperception that the stock market is a gambling casino. Now, of course, if you approach it that way, the stock market could be a gambling casino. And many people do approach this way by engaging in speculation such as day trading stocks to earn fast profits. We won't get into that here, but it goes without saying that most people are not disciplined enough to make money from those kinds of activities. The reality is most people trying to make quick cash in the stock market. But the fact that many people do succeed at such activities always keeps those dreams of making fast money in a day or two alive.

Of course, if you're interested in dividends, you are a more realistic and sensible person when it comes to handling money. You realize that investment and not speculation is the time-tested and true way to grow your money over the long-term. The fact is the long-term investors who buy-and-hold and don't panic always come out ahead.

The great depression and the 2008 financial crisis both illustrate why it is stupid to panic and pull your money out of the stock market during downturns. Let's look at the 2008 crash first. For our benchmark, we'll just use the Dow Jones industrial average. Although it's not the best benchmark probably, the valley of the Dow is what most people associate with the stock market, and of course, it does track with all the other indices.

According to the St. Louis Federal Reserve Bank, on July 10, 2009, the Dow Jones industrial average was 8146. Two years later, it was already over 12,000. The market had already grown by about 54% at that time.

By the time Pres. Obama was about to leave office in late December 2016, the Dow Jones industrial average was about 19,700 points. So, since that first date we quoted, the stock market had basically grown about 142%.

Now, those are some returns. Hopefully, our readers are aware that you can buy index funds that track major stock market indices. So, imagine what your money could've done investing just in the Dow Jones industrial average over that time span.

Now, of course, we are not trying to peddle the idea that this kind of growth is always going to happen. The point of this exercise is only to illustrate that recessions, even major ones, are temporary events. The overall growth of the economy and the capital in the economy is something that is a constant growth factor, and that's been proven over a very long period.

So, we can even see this in the mother of all recessions, the great depression of the 1930s. In July 1929, the stock market was experiencing an unprecedented rise in value. It was nearing the 5000-mark at that time.

That is incredible given that the economy was much smaller back then. By the summer of 1932, the market has dropped all the way down to about 842 points. Now, that seems dismal and it was. There were many factors that led to this; one of the most important was the Smoot-Hawley tariff act, which nearly single-handedly killed global trade. The Federal Reserve, which at that time had only been around for about 15 or 16 years, really didn't know how to handle the crisis. So, another factor that kept the depression going and worsened its effects is that the Federal Reserve severely reduced the money supply. Had these two events not happened to, add to the stock market crash, the Great Depression would've been much milder.

Those issues are for a discussion on another day. What's important for us is that from 1932 onwards, even though it was still a very difficult decade which included the rise of Adolf Hitler and Japan launching wars across Asia, the stock market experience great rebounds after 1932. Four years after Franklin Delano Roosevelt had been elected; the stock market had risen by 236%. Now, of course, I wasn't alive in 1932, but if you would have advised people in the summer of 1932 that the best thing they could do was to invest in the stock market, they would've thought you were completely crazy. And yet those people that did invest would have seen amazing returns.

We don't want to get too caught up in this, the point you should take away from this is that even the most drastic shocks to the stock market are temporary and are followed by great rebounds.

Another thing to consider is that things don't grind to a complete halt during economic downturns. For those who have lost their jobs, if they don't have any life savings, of course, an economic downturn is a major crisis. And yet, there are still massive amounts of economic activity going on. Even during the depression when unemployment rates reached record levels, most people were still employed. The same holds true for the 2008 financial crisis. If you avoid the temptation of looking at the size of the economy in relative terms comparing it to just a few years earlier which is what a recession actually does and look at it in absolute terms, even in the depths of the 2008 financial crisis, the United States economy was absolutely huge. Don't get me wrong, I'm not trying to downplay the huge problems that there were and the necessity to deal with them. But remember this. Even during an economic downturn, people need to get their prescription drugs, they still watch television, they are still using electricity, and they're still buying basic goods like toilet paper and food. So, here's a hint. A company like Walgreens which is an old established company based on providing vital daily goods is well-placed to survive an economic crisis.

All right, we spent enough time on this detour. But I hope that for those who are leery of the stock market, that is an objective review of some of the data makes them feel a little bit more relaxed about placing their money in the stock market. In the next section, I'm going to go over a couple of general strategies that will help you avoid getting financially destroyed by the fortunes of one single company or a single sector of the economy.

The Importance of Diversification

One of the most important strategies any investor in the stock market can use is diversification. Many people understand this to mean that you will take your money and put it in maybe 20 stocks or something like that. That kind of gets the idea. However, it doesn't go nearly far enough. But I don't mind mentioning it multiple times because it's so important. So, let me say this, putting your stock in 20 different companies is the bare minimum that you want to do in order to protect your capital. These days, we're only left with the choices of protecting our capital in nominal value by putting it in a bank or investing in bonds, contrasted with putting it at risk in the stock market. I think, by now, you're convinced that putting your capital in the bank or in bonds is something a little more attractive than bearing it in your backyard. With that in mind, that means we need a strategy where we can protect our money by taking advantage of the growth of the stock market.

And, of course, a major theme of this book, is also to take advantage of dividend payments for income, and moreover, seeking dividend payments that are growth oriented. So, in the end, you really don't need a bank account except for emergency savings. And let me do my duty at this point and encourage you to put a great deal of effort into building a small savings account to help you weather problems that may arise in your life. If you don't have a savings account or if you do and there's hardly any money in it, I recommend that you make a goal of getting $20,000 into that savings account. Now, you don't have to do that all at once, but set a goal that is at most 24-36 months out, to put regular monthly deposits into your savings account. After that, just leave it alone, unless it's a true emergency.

A Brief Look at Compound Interest

Anytime that you learn something new, you need to become familiar with the definitions of that niche or industry. First, let's recognize that dividend investing really has two goals.

The first goal is to leverage the stock market and the capital appreciation that it provides in order to grow our wealth over time. Many large and stable companies are obviously not going to be growing as fast as the hottest new stocks like Amazon, Netflix, or Google. However, they are going to be growing and probably much faster than inflation. When it comes to the stock market, many people have a shortsighted viewpoint. They have a Time window in mind that is short-term and so they are always looking at the ups and downs that take place over a year or two or even day-to-day. But that is not the correct way to look at it if you are a serious investor. You need to look at what happens to your money over long time frames. So, let's consider a 23-year time period to see what happened to Walgreens stock prices. For the record, Walgreens isn't exactly the best stock. But in 1996, it was about eight dollars a share. At the time that I am writing this, Walgreens is about $30 a share. So, its value has grown by 275%. If you had bought $10,000 worth of shares in 1996, you would have about 1,250 shares that would be worth $37,500 today. And we are imagining that you just bought the shares and didn't keep investing.

If you're going to compare that to what would happen to your money in a bank, you're going to find that the bank is hardly worth anything at all in comparison. Let's use a 20-year United States Treasury bond as an example of current interest rates. Right now, according to the St. Louis Federal Reserve Bank, the interest rate on a 20-year treasury bond is 2.8%. If you invested $10,000 into something that had an interest rate of 2.8% that was constant, after 20 years, you would have a little more than $17,000. That's a lot less than you would have by buying stock in Walgreens. So, here is a graph that I created at Smart asset.com showing how your money would've grown if you invested $10,000 into something that paid 2.8% interest and assuming you put no additional money:

To be completely honest, I'm not sure why anyone would even consider this. Inflation is going to wipe out all your gains. Now, of course, having $17,372 in the year 2038 would be a little better than going into your backyard and digging out the original $10,000, which we assume you protected by putting in a treasure chest. But if you were putting your money into Walgreens, as crazy as it sounds, you would be far better off. And we haven't even considered the fact that Walgreens pays dividends on top of the growth that it experiences in the stock market. And probably more to the point, there are many stocks that you can choose that are far better than Walgreens.

What is a Dividend?

So, now, let's turn our attention more directly to the topic of the book. The first thing we should make sure that everyone understands is what a dividend is. Simply put, a dividend is a share of the profits of the company for the previous quarter paid to stockholders in cash. The share that you're provided is obviously proportional to the number of shares of stock in the company that you own. Typically, the amount of the dividend is calculated as a percentage per share. Dividends are paid out on a quarterly basis. As we will see later, you can earn dividend income buying individual stocks or by buying into a fund like an exchange-traded fund. A great approach to investing is to have a portfolio that contains a little bit of both. As far as mutual funds, there is no reason to invest in mutual funds anymore. Mutual funds have a strict disadvantage in the high fees that they charge and the fact that they only trade once per day after hours. Exchange-traded funds give you all the benefits of mutual funds but without all the hassles and expensive fees. They trade just like stocks so you can buy and sell them at will on your own.

- **How to Pick Dividends**

Similar to nearly everything else in life, there is no magic key to tell you exactly how to pick the winning dividend – that key would be almost as good as a lottery tracker that would tell you the exact number to choose, but there are certain things that you can do to make sure that you are picking the right dividends and that you are getting the right money from the dividends that you have chosen. It is a good idea to make sure that you are picking everything in the right way so that, when the time comes, you can truly cash in on the dividends. Choosing the right ones will allow you to do so more quickly and will give you the chance to make even more money.

Profits in Company

The profits of the company are the number one thing that you should look at when you are deciding whether to choose them for your dividend investment. A company needs to have high profits for you to choose them and they need to show that they are going to have these profits for a long time in the future. It is a great way to make sure that the profits are going the right direction and to make sure that you are going to be able to make money off the investment that you make.

A company that has good profits is a good company.

Size of Payouts

You can always check the size of the payouts that the company has made in the past to find out what type of payments you can expect from the company. By simply looking at the trading profile of the company, you will be able to see how much they pay out, how often and what that takes out of the profits that they have made.

When you look at this amount, you need to consider all the aspects of the payouts. This also includes the initial investment amount. Compare that amount to what you are planning on investing in the company and see if the payouts will be worth it for what you are going to invest in the company. It is important to make sure that you are looking at all this information in a way as if you were going to invest in the company.

Health of Company

Just because a company has great profits and appears to be healthy does not mean that they are going to continue to be healthy. One of the most popular cases to look at is the case of Whole Foods Market. They are a huge company that has a lot of help from the people who shop there and the profits that they make. They did well when the crunchy organic movement was happening, but since the recession hit, their health has failed drastically. They are no longer profiting in the way that they would have been.

When you are considering an investment, consider the future health of the company. Just because it is profiting now, will it be profiting five years in the future? In general, a company that is trendy or one that is relatively new will not be able to offer healthy profits in the future because of the way that things are being done with the company and because it is difficult for the company to understand that they are not going to do as well as what they once thought they were going to be able to do.

History of Problems

No matter what you look at with the company, you need to always look at the history of the company. Ask yourself some questions:

•Do they have any blemishes in their history?

•What have they done in the past?

•Do they do a lot of business on a regular basis?

•Are they affected by the seasons?

Each of these questions will tell you what you need to know about the history of the company and the way that they worked in the past.

In investing, it is not uncommon for history to repeat itself so if a company had issues in the past, there is a high chance that they will have issues in the future. Keep this in mind when you are investing in the company and even when you are just researching the options that you have when it comes to investing in the company.

By looking at the history portfolio of the company, you will be able to make sure that you are getting the most out of the experience and that you are going to see what is going on with the company so that you can make more important decisions about the future.

Some Tips

What would a helpful book about dividend investing be without some quick tips on companies that are among the best to choose? While these are going to pay you only a small amount of dividend payments, they are the ones that are going to be steady and stable for a long period of time. If you are hoping to make money from these companies, you can always invest more money into it so that you can get higher payments.

The top companies to choose a dividend investment plan from are Wal-Mart, Target, Dr. Pepper, and Hershey. They are companies that have high profits and relatively high payouts. While it is impossible to tell you that you should choose a company to invest in (and illegal in most areas), having an idea of what these companies are all about can help you make the decision on your own whether or not you want to choose the company.

Be sure that you choose a company that works with you because that is what you want. Don't choose to invest your money in a company because a book told you to or someone else told you to. Do your own research, learn about the companies and figure out exactly what you want to get out of the investment opportunity.

Chapter 19 Buying Dividend Growth Stocks for Retirement

Now that you know exactly what to look for in companies to consider purchasing for your dividend growth portfolio, it's time to implement the plan. Let's begin putting your dividend growth portfolio together.

In the above process, you should have created your dividend growth stock watch list and come up with a group of at least 25 companies that you would like to invest in. You've reviewed the financial data from these companies and determined that you believe them to be solid companies worthy of your investment dollars. Now it's time to go shopping.

Earlier we calculated the amount of money you need to save on a monthly basis in order to reach your retirement goals. Ideally, after contributing enough in your 401K account to get the full company match, you have more savings left to put into an IRA or taxable brokerage account. The IRA or brokerage account is where you will do your dividend growth investing.

So, each month you are going to contribute a set amount into your dividend growth account (IRA or taxable account). As this money accumulates in your account, it is time to begin purchasing dividend growth stocks from the watch list you created.

Your goal is to eventually own a portfolio of at least 25 dividend growth companies. But you must begin with your first purchase.

In order to keep trading costs low, I recommend that you make your purchases in a minimum of $1,000 increments. If you are paying a $7 commission, this will equate to 0.7% (7/1,000 = 0.007) trading expense for each purchase you make. We want to try to keep our trading costs below 1% so that not too much of our money is being wasted on an unnecessary expense.

So, when you have your first $1,000 saved up in your account, it is time to make your first purchase. What you want to do is a quick review of your stock watch list. Remember, you should have already done a more in-depth review of these companies and determined that they are good enough for you to invest in long term. If you haven't gone through the company evaluation process described earlier, make sure to go back and go through the process as it is very important to make sure you are investing in high quality companies in order to give you the greatest chance of retirement success.

Review your stock watch list quickly by looking at the P/E ratios (price/earnings) of each company on your list. The P/E ratio is an easy valuation method you can use to quickly get an idea if a company is currently trading at a low price, a fair price or too high of a price. The P/E ratio tells you how many dollars you will pay in price for each dollar of earnings the company has. So, for example, if a company is currently trading at a P/E ratio of 15, then you are paying $15 for each $1 in company profits. The lower the P/E ratio, the less you are paying for each dollar in profits.

Unfortunately, it isn't as easy as saying companies with lower P/E ratios are always the best to invest in. There are a few different factors that determine how the market might value a company. For example, companies with higher expected future growth will trade at a higher P/E ratio than a company that isn't expected to grow much in the future.

Historically, the companies making up the S&P 500 (a good benchmark of the stock market) trade at an average P/E ratio around 15. What this means is that when companies are trading at P/E ratios lower than 15, we can assume they are trading at a reasonable price. Companies trading at P/E's above 15 are possibly trading on the high side. However, this isn't a rule of thumb across the board. P/E ratios can vary between companies and industries depending on the future growth prospects.

When looking over your watch list to decide which company to purchase, there are a few things to take into consideration. First, I review what companies I already currently own. It is important to diversify your portfolio by owning many different companies (eventually you want to build a portfolio of at least 25 companies) and having exposure to companies in different industries. Next, I want to review the P/E ratios of the companies on my stock watch list. Usually, I will first focus on the companies that are trading with a lower P/E ratio because I would need to pay fewer dollars for each dollar in earnings to purchase them. When I find a company that interests me, I check over my current portfolio to see if I already own that company and if I currently have enough exposure to that company or industry compared to my portfolio in whole. If I already have enough exposure to that company or industry, I will seek out a different company on my watch list.

Eventually, my goal is to own a portfolio of at least 25 companies. In order to do this, and to stay properly diversified, I will spread my purchases around $1,000 to 25 different companies before I ever make a second purchase of any single company. By doing this I help keep my portfolio properly diversified.

Diversification of a portfolio is very important because it reduces the amount of risk we are taking with our investments. By diversifying, owning 25 different companies spread across multiple industries, we are reducing our risk of negative effects from one individual company or industry. For example, if in the future the tobacco industry begins to struggle, the negative effect won't put our portfolio into ruin because we made sure not to have too much exposure to any single industry. While the companies we own in that industry may suffer, the companies we own in other industries hopefully will do alright and negate any negative effects from the exposure to the tobacco industry.

Same goes with any one individual company. If you own Company ABC and they suddenly have huge negative news causing the stock price to plummet and Company ABC to cut their dividend, the impact shouldn't be too great on your portfolio that you cannot recover as long as you were properly diversified. In fact, if you own 25 different companies with roughly equal weightings, a complete loss from any one individual company would only have a negative 4% effect on your portfolio. When we are in retirement and relying on the passive dividend income from our portfolio, diversification becomes very important so that a bad effect from any one company we own won't completely sabotage our entire retirement.

So, what you want to do is begin building your dividend growth portfolio by purchasing $1,000 lots of each company that you've approved for your watch list. Begin with the lower trading companies based on P/E but make sure you make a purchase of each company on your watch list (at minimum 25, maximum 50) before making a repurchase of any one company. This will mean at times you will possibly be purchasing some companies that are trading at a higher P/E ratio than other companies that you already own. But we want to make sure we are properly diversifying our portfolio risk so the higher price you must pay for some companies becomes worth it.

One note though is that I generally will not purchase any security that is trading with a P/E above 22. Personally, I prefer to stick with companies trading with under 20 P/E's but I'm willing sometimes to bend the rules slightly as long as the purchase is improving the diversification of my portfolio and it is a good quality company that I want to own. If this is the case then I may occasionally make a purchase of a company with a P/E over 20, but never over 22.

Each month, you will put in your retirement savings account the amount you calculated that you need to be saving in order to give you the best chance of reaching your retirement goals. As you are putting your money aside, you will begin making purchases in $1,000 increments of the dividend growth companies you have included on your stock watch list. This is the process you will take over the long term until you reach your target retirement date.

Hopefully, if everything goes well, you will be able to successfully retire at your target date. You will have built up a substantial portfolio of dividend growth stocks that will be paying you a passive income in the form of dividends. Also, this income will continue to grow year after year as the companies you own increase the number of dividends they are paying out to shareholders.

Reinvesting Dividends

One of the benefits of investing in dividend stocks is that they will pay you a passive income in the form of dividends. Most companies will pay out to shareholders part of their earnings in the form of dividends each quarter. During retirement, you will be using this passive dividend income to live off. However, while you are still in the accumulation phase, still building your nest egg before you've reached retirement, it will be important to reinvest those dividends rather than spend them.

By reinvesting your dividends, you are saving even more money each year and accumulating even more dividend growth stocks. As time goes, your dividend income will grow allowing you to save more and more each year. This will be a huge bonus towards helping you reach your retirement goals.

There are a couple different ways you can go about reinvesting your dividend income.

The first and possibly most commonly followed way involves simply reinvesting the dividends back into the company that pays them. For example, if you own Coca-Cola stock and they pay you out $1,500 in dividends, you will simply buy new shares of Coca-Cola with that $1,500. That same quarter, your Procter & Gamble stock may pay you $1,300 in dividends and you will use that$1,300 to buy more shares of Procter & Gamble. This is the easiest way to go about reinvesting dividends because it requires little work on your part. The decision is easy to just use dividends from each company to buy more shares of that respective company. Some brokerages will even do this process automatically for you so that it is completely passive on your part.

The second way to reinvest dividends and the way that I currently follow involves a little more work but still easy to implement. The second way involves accumulating the dividend income in your account as cash. Then when you have enough cash, you can choose which company you want to use that cash to buy more shares of. I prefer to make my purchases in $1,000 increments in order to keep trading costs low. There are a couple benefits of this second method for reinvesting your dividends. The first is that it allows you to pick the best investment option at any given time. Rather than buying companies no matter what current valuation they are selling at, you can choose a reasonably valued company (based on P/E ratio) to purchase. The second benefit is that you can help balance out your portfolio with these purchases to keep proper diversification.

Keeping A Properly Balanced Portfolio

Earlier, we discussed the idea of diversification and why you want to keep a properly diversified portfolio. You want to try to build your portfolio to at least own a minimum of 25 different companies with a good mix of industries. This will allow your portfolio to recover easily from any negative effects from any single company or industry.

There are a couple ways to go about keeping a properly balanced (diversified) portfolio.

I would recommend that on an annual basis you check the total diversification of your portfolio. In order to do this, you will first list out all your companies. Take the value of the stock of each individual company dividend by your total account value. This will give you the percentage that you hold in each individual company. Make sure that not a single company has too high of a percentage.

If you own 25 stocks, then each company should have around 4% invested in it (give or take a couple percent). You can calculate how much to have invested in each company by taking 100 dividends by the total amount of companies you own. So, if you own 40 companies, then each stock should make up about 2.5% of our portfolio (give or take a couple percent).

Notice I'm not too much of a stickler on this rule. It would always be nearly impossible to keep a perfectly balanced portfolio. The main point is that you want to make sure no single company is putting you at too much risk. Personally, I would try to keep the exposure of any one company to less than 5% of your portfolio.

If you monitor your portfolio diversification annually, you will often find that it is slightly out of balance. There are a couple ways you can go about fixing this issue.

The first method works well while you are still building your nest egg and before you have a large portfolio (in dollars) built up. In the first method, you can simply bring your portfolio back in balance through the year by purchasing shares of companies that your portfolio is underweight in. For example, if you own too much Coca-Cola but not very much Procter & Gamble, then you can fix this problem through the year by purchasing more shares of Procter & Gamble and buying no new shares of Coca-Cola. This method can help bring your portfolio back into a better balance and is easy to accomplish if the size of your portfolio is not yet too large.

The second method will have to be used when your portfolio has reached a larger size. Sometimes it will be nearly impossible to bring your portfolio back into better balance simply by purchasing the underweighted companies. So, what you will possibly need to do is sell some shares of the overweight companies (companies that make up too high a percentage of your portfolio) and use the proceeds to purchase the underweighted companies. You will want to be careful when doing this to sell off only the number of shares you need to bring that overweight company down to a more reasonable percentage of your portfolio.

For example, let's assume you test your diversification and you find that Coca-Cola makes up 10% of your portfolio. Let's assume your total portfolio consists of 35 companies so a properly diversified portfolio would have a little less than 3% invested in each company. So, you need to reduce your Coca-Cola exposure down close to 3%. What you will want to do is sell out of 70% of your Coca-Cola shares and invest that money back into the companies that you are currently underweight in. In order to calculate how much of a company, you need to sell, simply take the current percentage you own and subtract out the goal percentage you want to own (10-3=7). You will then take the result and divide by the original percentage you owned (7/10=0.70 or 70%). This gives you the amount you need to trim your position by.

The other thing you will want to track is the diversification of specific industries. You can do this the same way by adding up the value of all your stocks from one specific industry and then dividing by the total portfolio value. I would recommend trying to keep your exposure to any one industry at 8% or less. The lower the better but there are some industries that offer a great deal of dividend growth companies (mainly oil, tobacco and consumer products) which you will probably have more exposure to.

You can fix an industry related diversification problem the same way that you would a company related diversification problem.

The goal is to keep a properly balanced portfolio so that negative effects (dividend cut, company related problems, industry downturn) from any company or industry will not drastically harm your portfolio. A properly diversified portfolio will carry you along towards your retirement goals and through your retirement years with less risk involved.

When You May Need to Sell a Company

Dividend growth investors should be long term investors. This means that when you purchase stocks, you are planning on owning for a very long time. In some cases, you may own some companies your entire life once you make your first purchase.

However, there will be times when you need to sell a company. Companies are in business of course and sometimes business does not always go perfectly as planned.

There are a few reasons you may need to sell out of one of your dividend growths stocks.

1.   Change in company fundamentals. When you reviewed the companies, you want to invest in, you are reviewing the fundamental metrics of the company. You reviewed the sales revenues, net profits and earnings per share. You also reviewed the strength of the balance sheet. At the time, these metrics met your criteria, so you added the company to your watch list and eventually purchased shares. However,

sometimes companies falter. Sometimes business turns south, competitive landscapes change, and the company is no longer operating as good as it used to. You will need to periodically review the fundamentals of the companies you own (best to do annually but every couple year can suffice) in order to make sure everything is still going as expected with company operations. If you see a problem (earnings become erratic, drop in profitability, too much debt, etc.) then you might decide it is time to sell out of the company and buy one with brighter prospects.

2.   Failure to Increase Dividend Rate. You are a dividend growth investor. You invest in dividend growth stocks because not only do they pay you a passive income, but that passive income grows each year to outpace inflation (which is a very important benefit during retirement). Dividend growth investors want to own companies that increase their dividend rate every single year. Sometimes, management will be forced to make the decision not to increase the dividend payment to shareholders each year. Usually

this is a signal of trouble and most dividend growth investors will take this as a sign to cut ties (sell the stock) and move on to one of the many other companies still growing dividends. You should consider the tax consequences of a sale in this situation. If you have huge unrealized gains, then a sale will take a large portion of those gains as taxes. In this case, you may decide to give the company some time to see what they will do with the dividend over the next year or two. If a company goes more than 2 years in a row without a dividend increase, I would strongly encourage considering a sell and purchase of a different company that is still growing their dividend.

3.   Decrease of the dividend rate. At times, management will be forced to cut their dividend. This usually signals trouble ahead. Most dividend growth investors will take this as a sign of trouble and immediately sell this company in order to purchase shares of a company still growing their dividend. One of the last things management of a dividend growth company wants to do is cut their dividend. If they have

a long dividend growth streak going, then a cut in a dividend will signal that management is concerned about the near- or long-term future of the company. Take a dividend cut as a sell signal and get out. There are plenty of great companies still growing their dividends that you can buy in its place.

Chapter 20 Analyzing Dividend Stocks

An Example of Switching Stocks

Sanofi-Aventis (SNY) is a large, high quality French drug company stock that I bought at the market bottom in March 2009. This stock was listed in both of Value Line's model dividend-oriented portfolios. The low purchase price gave me a 5.6% yield for a dividend that was paid once each year in June. The share price came up about 50% by November 2009 as did the market indexes and at that price the yield became a little over 3%. The share price rise during the previous several weeks seemed to have hit a "resistance level." It was still a stock well worth owning, but would I want to buy it at the latest price if I had not already owned it? If I sold, could I find a replacement that was a better investment? As I had accumulated so many capital losses during early 2009, a short-term gain on (SNY) would not change my tax situation for 2009 or for many future years.

Eli Lilly (LLY) is an American drug company stock of a slightly higher quality level than Sanofi-Aventis (SNY).

The (LLY) share price offered a dividend yield that was 40% higher than the (SNY) yield. Equally important, the price earnings ratio (P/E) for (LLY) was historically lower at 8 dues to the temporary absence of new products in development. Other, smaller differences in the attractiveness of (LLY) over (SNY) were a higher financial strength rating, almost double the net profit per employee for (LLY) and a higher projected total annual return. This tax free, higher dividend switch made sense and is an example of improving your portfolio and dividend income by monitoring your portfolio at least once per month.

Share Price Ratios and Rates

Price earnings ratios (P/E) will vary for many reasons, among which are fear and greed, investor sentiment, competing interest rates on bonds and CDs, earnings growth rates, earnings stability, history of the stock's reliability, earnings predictability and other factors.

A dividend investor should have a limit in mind as to the highest acceptable P/E ratio. This need not be as firm as the setting of a minimal dividend yield, but you still need a sensible guide, even one needing an occasional adjustment. A P/E of 16 is about as high as I care to go at the present time for the typical dividend paying stock. On the other hand, capital gains-oriented growth investors often pay 20-30 times earnings for a hot growth stock. However, history teaches that rapid growth has limits over the long haul and earnings growth of the size needed to support high P/E ratios are unsustainable. Ignore growth stocks and their extra risks as well as their lack of offering a steady and adequate dividend income.

When examining the 10-15-year history of average annual P/E ratios for a stock in Value Line's survey sheet, you are looking at the parameters of the opinions of the investment community as to the value of that stock. Buying a stock at the lowest P/E ratio in its historical range almost ensures that you will get your money back if things don't work out or you discover a better spot for your funds.

To lessen your risk further, check Value Line's "earnings predictability" rating in the lowest right-hand corner of the survey sheet. This rating should be at least 50. Read across the "earnings per share" and "cash flow per share" in the historical guide in the upper one half of the sheet. Cash flow is what supports the dividend. Deep drop offs in these figures and deficits should be a concern regarding the objective of your search - a sustainable, growing dividend. Even the best of businesses occasionally has short periods of bad times.

Dividend growth is ultimately dependent upon the growth of earnings and cash flow. All these should keep up with inflation, at the least. Ideally, earnings growth rates of 6-15% are what the dividend investor wants, but occasionally a lower than inflation earnings growth rate is acceptable if the long history proves that the firm is of the highest quality and the dividend yield is fairly high (example; Consolidated Edison in 2009).

An interesting fact about the variability of P/E ratios during a crash from a bull market is that from 1929-

1932 the P/E ratio of the market varied from 33 down to 6. Very low P/Es usually signal opportunities to buy some stocks at exceptionally low prices, otherwise known as "screaming buys." Other signals for these "screaming buys" can be P/E below the return on shareholder equity and that the earnings growth % rate plus dividend yield % divided by the P/E ratio equals one or more.

Return on shareholder equity is another measure worth considering. Whatever measures you check on the firm's Value Line survey sheet, be sure to compare them with industry comments and measures located at the start of the survey section for the firm's business sector. There you will find industry wide information and perhaps a more complete perspective.

There are other share price ratios that the investor may wish to check such as price/book value, price/revenue, price/cash flow, price to funds from operations in the case of REITs. But, given the guidelines covered at this point in the book, I don't believe going into too many details will be beneficial. P/E ratios are by far the most important. Scientific analysis of the decision-making process points out the dangers of too much information and how it infringes upon our ability to think clearly. Nonetheless, you can read across the historical figures on the survey sheets at all the lines where a dangerous trend could be spotted in revenues, capital spending, net profit, long term debt, etc.

Other Factors to Consider

Too much debt has ruined many businesses. Many advisors recommend debt to be no more than 60% of total capital, but certain industries such as utilities can safely have more debt. If you are an accountant, you may glean much from the annual report that you can thoroughly understand. Value Line solves the problem for us non-accountants with their survey figures on how earnings cover long term interest, total debt, histories of long-term debt (check the trend) long term debt ratio, company's financial strength and safety ratings. If a stock carries a high financial strength rating and a safety rating of one, the investor need look no further. But if the stock carries a safety rating of 3 and a financial strength rating below A, you should look deeper at interest coverage and other debt items.

Over the decades small cap stocks have had a higher rate of total return over mid and large caps but there is more risk involved, information is more difficult to obtain, and dividends may be low or non-existent; not good prospects for the dividend investor. I rarely own any small caps. I am much more inclined towards blue chip stocks. One definition of a blue chip is a stock which had 5 or more dividend increases in the past 12 years; the highest overall quality rating; at least 5 million shares; at least 80 institutional investors; at least 25 years of uninterrupted dividends and earnings increases in 7 of the last 12 years. Any good company could grow at least at the rate of the sum of the percentage cost of their borrowings plus the rate of inflation.

Be wary of a company that desires to acquire another large firm. Very often they pay too much for the acquired firm and the acquisition is often driven by top management whose goal is to have more businesses under their control to justify another increase in their already higher than necessary salaries. On the other hand, if the stock you own is the target of another firm's desire to acquire, you will probably be offered a high price for your shares. Take their offer, sell and don't get involved as a shareholder in the acquiring firm.

Outside forces will have one of the greatest effects on the price of shares you own or wish to own: the general stock market can drive prices up or down for no apparent reason, high interest rates can bring share prices down and lower rates can bring share prices up and inflation rates, or the anticipation of a change in rates, can drive P/E rates from an average of 9 when inflation is quite high to P/E rates of 17 when inflation is under 2.5%

Finally, stay with companies that produce a product or service for which most people can envision a long-term demand. Do your own homework of analysis and don't rely on the forecasts of professional analysts. Buy stocks that you can live with in the coming years. The

Warren Buffett approach to selecting companies, that is looking at a company as if you were considering buying the entire firm, is a great approach to keep in mind. Mr. Buffett prefers very large firms that are involved in simple, understandable business, offering the power of consistent earnings with sensible limits of debt and whose share prices are low enough to provide a margin of safety.

Chapter 21 Dividend yield

Not all, but many companies that pay a high dividend also have a high payout ratio.

Verizon Payout Ratio

Verizon has a 5.03% dividend yield and an average payout ratio of 90%. This means that they payout 90% of their earnings out to shareholders in the form of dividends.

They have been growing their dividend at a rate of 2.9% over the last years. 2.9% is not flattering, but one benefit with high dividend-yielding stocks is that you get a higher dividend income upfront that you can use to reinvest or buy other stocks.

So, what is better, higher yield low growth or lower yield high growth? I lean toward lower yield faster growth, but honestly, I have both in my investment portfolio.

Keep in mind, however, that if the economy goes through a slump and stock prices start declining across the board, many stocks will have a high yield. This is the optimal scenario to buy great companies and receive a high yielding dividend.

Many companies with a competitive advantage can increase their dividends without having to sell more products or services or find new customers to sell to, even if their customer base is small.

For example, a company that sells potato chips sells an 8 oz. bag for $1. They have a customer base of 100,000 people that love their potato chips. Every customer just buys one bag, which gives this company a total revenue of $100k. Total expenses for one bag end up being 80 cents, which leaves the company a net income of $20,000 (20 cents x 100,000 bags sold).

The company decides to pay out a 50% dividend, so shareholders receive a total of $10,000 in dividends.

The following year's cost per bag has gone up to 90 cents, the company decides to pass the cost on to its customers and sells the same 8 oz. bag for $1.15. They still have the same customer base that buys one bag. Now their total revenue is $115,000. The company's net income is $25,000. They stick with the 50% payout ratio and end up paying $12,500 total in dividends. The company was able to increase its dividend by 25%, without having acquired new customers or selling more potato chip bags.

So, whenever you go into your local grocery store and notice that the prices on your favorite products have increased, now you know why.

Companies with a competitive advantage can raise their prices year after year and raise the dividends they pay out, without acquiring new customers.

We've looked at a couple of metrics that can be used to analyze a company. Are these the only metrics? No, but these performance metrics give you a high-level overview of how the company is performing. If anything seems off, I can always dive in deeper and comb through the financial statements. This, however, is something that I rarely do; because that's way too boring.

I just stick to the high-level metrics, because anything that might affect performance in a bad way will filter to the top and I will notice it either by the P/E ratio dropping, the price of the stock tumbling, weak earnings report, dip in revenue or net income, high debt level or any other bad circumstances that could pop up.

I also lean on a company's competitive advantage pulling it out of any business turmoil it might go through and I keep an eye on the 5 to 10 years performance.

How much to pay

You go to your local grocery store and you see your favorite chocolate candy bar selling for $3, you are used to buying it cheaper than $3, so you decide not to purchase it that day.

You go back to the store after one week and you notice that the price of the same chocolate candy bar is now on sale for $1. You freak out and start loading up on chocolate candy bars because you've never seen it this cheap.

That's the same way you are going to be buying dividend stocks when you can get them at a deep discount. How much you pay for a stock depends on the value of the stock itself. You don't just buy a stock because you like the company. You should only buy if the stock is trading at a deep discount compared to its value.

Right now, Walmart has a market cap of $189 billion and Chevron has a market cap of $167 billion. If I gave you $190 billion today and told you to buy the company that's the better deal, which one would you buy? Why?

Would you buy Chevron because it looks cheaper compared to Walmart? Always look at buying stocks as if you're buying the whole company. If you take that perspective, you will be more diligent in your research on deciding which company's stock to buy.

Also, if you wouldn't buy the whole company if you had the capital, don't even think about buying even one share in the company.

To figure out which of the two companies we would like to buy and how much we want to pay for it, we need to decide the value of a company first. There are two ways: book value or net income.

The book value is the tangible worth of the company and this is also what shareholders would get if the company gets liquidated (sold). Book value is calculated as assets – liabilities. Book value may look like shareholders equity, but it only contains tangible assets that can be sold. Intangible assets like goodwill or brand recognition cannot be sold.

Net income is the second and my most favorite way of valuing a company. The amount of income a company generates tells me how much I am willing to pay for it. Since we are looking to invest in profitable businesses that should not get liquidated, we will use the net income method of valuing a business.

Let's scale it back a little bit with a fun short story. A group of kids in your neighborhood are very assertive and entrepreneurial. They started their own lemonade business, where they've set up lemonade stands in the local community.

All year round they meet plenty of thirsty customers and they can generate $10,000 in net profit. They sell lemonade for 50 cents a glass and make 25 cents profit. So, they are selling more than 100 glasses a day to reach that $10k profit.

After doing this for a year, they are getting tired of standing outside in rain, sleet or snow and would rather be sitting at home playing video games all day (games they bought with their lemonade money of course).

You offer to buy the lemonade business from them and have your nephews running the day to day operations. They got in a huddle and did some quick math.

If the lemonade business makes them $10,000 a year profit, it would be foolish to sell it for less than that amount, because they will have incurred a major loss. If they sell it for $10,000, they haven't made any profit, because they can do those numbers in a year.

All things being equal, if their expenses and profit stay the same year after year, they decide to sell the business for $100,000, which is 10 years' worth of profits. So, the young entrepreneurs decided on $100,000, they think that amount will buy them video games for a lifetime.

Now you, on the other hand, want to get the business as cheap as possible. If you can get it for $5,000 you will be up 100% the first year. Because you spend $5,000 and the business generated $10,000. If you can buy their business for $10,000, you are also a winner, because you will have made your money back in just one year. Everything after year one is just pure profit.

You were eventually able to negotiate the price down to $50,000, which means that you will make all your money back in year 5 or a 20% immediate return of your investment ($10,000/$50,000). After year five, everything you earn is just pure profit and you can use the money to buy a different business.

There is a specific formula that investors use, called the P/E ratio. It shows you how much money you pay for $1 profit a company generates. P stands for price and E stands for earnings.

We paid $50,000 (P) for the lemonade company and the company had a net income, or earnings, of $10,000 (E). So, you take the earnings and divide that by the price to get the P/E ratio: $50,000/$10,000 = 5. For every 5 dollars, you spend you bought one dollar in profit.

The same way we valued the young entrepreneurs' lemonade business is the same way we will evaluate the big businesses on the stock market, like Walmart and Chevron. Don't forget that when we invest, we are looking at our initial return and how many years it will take to get our original investment back.

We're going to do two things, we're taking the market cap of the companies, which is the total value of the company on the stock market and break it down to a single share price and we will take the net income and break it down to income for a single share.

The market cap for Walmart is $189 billion, they have 3.20 billion shares outstanding, so to break it down to a single share price we take: $189 billion / 3.20 billion shares outstanding = $59.08.

$59.08, is also the price that you will see on the stock market when people are talking about the share price of Walmart.

Walmart generated $14.912 billion in net income. To break it down to one share we take $14.912 billion / 3.20 billion shares outstanding = $4.66. This $4.66 is the net income per share, but investors also call it earnings per share (EPS). The earnings per share are nothing more than the total net income divided by shares outstanding.

Now to get to our P/E ratio, we take our EPS and divide that by the price: $59.08/$4.66= 12.68. For every $12.68 you spend you bought $1 in Walmart profit.

Another way to look at it is you had an initial 7.9% initial rate of return ($1/$12.68), or if Walmart made the same income year after year, it would take 12.68 years to get your investment money back.

As an investor you want to get your initial investment back as fast as possible, that's why you should only buy companies that have a low P/E ratio.

But what is a low P/E ratio? It depends on the stock market, the economy, the industry your company is in, and on the average P/E the company has been trading in the past years.

I've noticed that most companies I keep an eye on are trading at a P/E ranging from 7 to 75. Most investors like buying companies that are trading at a P/E of 20 or less. I only buy companies trading at a P/E of 15 or less.

Whenever the economy is prospering and people feel optimistic, they spend money more freely and the stock market reflects this behavior. Companies start trading at higher P/E ratios of 30 and up because investors bid up the price of the stock. This is when the market is overvalued.

For example, company ABC is selling for $100 a share and has earnings of $4, for a P/E ratio of 25. Investors start bidding up the price of the stock to $140. The earnings are still at $4, which gives us a P/E ratio of 35. This to me is too high of a P/E ratio, like I said earlier I only buy at P/E ratios of 15 or less.

The opposite also holds true, whenever the economy tanks, like during the great depression, people get pessimistic about the economy and start selling their stocks and investments because they feel like the sky is falling.

The stock market goes up and everybody jumps on the bandwagon and bids up the prices of stocks. The stock market is overvalued, and the bubble is about to burst. Then the stock market tanks or corrects itself and everybody tries to jump off the ship and tries to save themselves, now the market is undervalued.

So, in this case company ABC went from $140 a share at its peak and tumbled down to $130, $119, $101, $80, $58, and then to $40. If earnings per share is still at $4, now the P/E ratio is at 10.

Everybody tried to get out of the market as quickly as possible because stock prices were falling. You will now see P/E ratios in the single digits.

It is at this moment that I shift into second gear and start buying companies like my life depended on it. I'm like a kid in a candy store and the owner tells me that I can have all the candy I can put my hands on in the next 30 minutes.

Remember, it's the shareholders who trade these stocks back and forth. The underlying company still is fundamentally sound and will generate profits and dividends for its shareholders.

Also, most investors don't trade their stocks frequently. The average volume of shares that have been trading daily for Walmart stock is about 11.72 million, compared to 3.20 billion shares outstanding. That is

0.37% of total shares that are trading daily. The other 99.63% of shares are owned by investors who just sit on their shares and collect the dividend.

Walmart P/E was under 15 in 2009. Also, with a lower P/E ratio I can buy more stocks, which will give me more dividends.

If I had $2,000 to spend and I bought company ABC at $140 a share I would only be able to buy 14 whole shares, but if I bought the company at $40 a share, I would have bought 50 shares. Instead of getting 14 cash dividends, I now get 50 cash dividends.

Going back to our Walmart vs Chevron example, it would be tedious to constantly have to calculate the market cap, share price, P/E ratio, and EPS. Luckily most of this information is readily available and you can just look at the P/E ratio without having to think about the calculation.

Walmart Investment Metrics. Source: Google Finance

For example, Google Finance already has these numbers calculated for you. You can also add all the dividend calculations if you want to. Let's skip calculating Chevron's EPS and P/E ratio and let's just pull it from our online source.

Chevron Investment Metrics. Source: Google Finance

Based on the P/E ratios alone I would buy Walmart instead of Chevron.

Keep in mind that dividends are paid out of earnings and if you look at both Walmart and Chevron you see that Chevron is paying a higher dividend. Without looking at other factors, I would still buy Walmart over Chevron.

When to sell

You will hear good news about a company and the stock price will reflect this by going up. You will also hear bad news because a company might have missed its quarterly projected earnings by a few pennies and the stock price will tumble down or there might be some so-called financial expert who will tell you to buy a stock because it's about to sign a major contract which will boost sales.

It's best not to pay too much attention to all this noise and focus on the financial data.

When it comes to selling stocks, I only sell if a company stops paying the dividend, the company fundamentally changes for the worse, or if the dividend has not kept up with inflation.

If a company stops paying dividends, it tells me that the business is in financial trouble and I need to investigate. Companies keep their shareholders happy when they pay out dividends constantly. It's a major problem if the company stops paying out dividends, the stock will most likely also drop in price.

Not too long ago, I broke some of my own rules when it comes to buying dividend stocks and purchased stocks in a company called American Realty Capital Properties (ARCP). This was a monthly dividend-paying company, but it did not have at least a 10-year track record of paying increased dividends.

I received my first dividend when the pay date arrived, but the following dividends never arrived.

Management at ARCP was cooking the books and when this was found out all hell broke loose. The dividend was eliminated, senior management left the company, and shareholders were angry.

Throughout this whole debacle, the stock price continued to decline, and it took a new management team and a change of company name to bring the company back on track.

The company ended up reinstated its dividend 10 months after paying the last one. Looking back, I could've invested the money in a better way. But whenever you make a mistake and believe me you will make mistakes, just learn from it and move on. No use crying over spilled milk.

Sometimes companies fundamentally change by neglecting what they are good at or known for and instead jump into a new market. If a company you invested in is in the chocolate chip cookies selling business and all of a sudden jumps into fashion design and puts all of its energy and resources in building that up, it might not be the best use of resources.

There are quite a few companies that buy out competitors or try something new. PepsiCo, for example, sells many different products. Besides the Pepsi soft drink, they also sell Lays potato chips, Quaker oatmeal, Doritos, and more. They have a wide assortment of products, but they stay in the consumer staples industry. They don't stray away from what they do best.

If a company has not been able to grow its dividend fast enough, you should either sell it or collect the dividend you receive and purchase other companies with it.

Whenever I am not buying companies at a P/E of 15 or less, I just sit back and collect dividends. Being patient and waiting for the right opportunities to buy is a skill.

If you follow the rules for selling dividend stocks, you will be able to tune out the noise. The worst thing you can do is constantly buy and sell your stocks because this will hurt your overall return.

Sitting still, not doing anything, and waiting for the right time to buy is a skill you will learn. Sometimes it can take months or years before you get the opportunity to buy a company you've been eyeing like a hawk at a low P/E ratio.

Chapter 22 The REIT

How Do You Define Real Estate Investment Trust 'REIT'?

A REIT is a security that sells like a stock on the major exchanges. You can invest in real estate directly or through real estate properties and mortgages. What makes Real Estate Investment Trusts so popular is the fact that they offer special tax considerations. Moreover, you can also get high yields as an investor. Remember, REITs are a highly liquid method of investing in real estate.

Here are a few terms you will come across when dealing with REITs.

1. Equity REITs

Equity REIT means you invest in and own a real estate property. You will only be responsible for the equity or value of your own real estate assets. Revenue in Real Estate Investment Trusts comes from property rents.

2. Mortgage REITs

As the name suggests, mortgage REITs deal mainly in investment and ownership of real estate property mortgages. These REITs lend money for mortgages and this loan is given to owners of real estate. The loan can be used to purchase existing mortgages or mortgage-backed securities.

Mortgage Real Estate Investment Trusts mainly generate revenue by the interest earned on the mortgage loans.

3. Hybrid REITs

This form of Real Estate Investment Trust combines the investment strategies of equity REITs and mortgage REITs. Hybrid REITs allow you to invest in both properties and mortgages.

How you can invest in Real Estate Investment Trust - REIT

You can invest in REITs either by purchasing shares from an open exchange directly or put your investment in a mutual fund that specializes in public real estate. Here is some more good news for you. You should think about investing in REITs because many of them are accompanied by other favorable investment options such as dividend reinvestment plans (DRIPs).

Among other things, Real Estate Investment Trusts invest in shopping malls, apartments, office buildings, hotels and warehouses. You can find REITs which invest only in one area of real estate – office buildings for example.

Some REITs only invest in one specific geographical region i.e. state or country. Remember, investing in real estate investment trusts is a dividend paying means of taking part in the real estate market.

How to do things the REIT way

There are plenty of investment options out there and this creates a challenge for most investors.

Things get interesting when you get a lot of advice from your friends. For most people, stocks are the core of successful investing. For some, bonds are the safest place to put money and others prefer to put their money in mutual funds.

Real Estate Investment Trusts are not as well-known as these categories and often, they are the most overlooked investment option.

So, what is a REIT company?

REIT Company accumulates a pool of money through IPO or Initial Public Offering. This IPO is then used to buy, manage, develop and sell real estate assets. If you compare IPO with other security offerings, it is identical in terms of reporting requirements and regulation.

The difference, however, is that instead of purchasing stocks from a single company, the REIT owner is buying a portion of the real estate pool. Yes, you can buy a portion of a managed pool of real estate even if you own one REIT unit. This pool will then generate income through leasing, renting and selling of property, which is distributed to you directly (i.e. the REIT owner) on a regular basis.

What are the advantages of buying a REIT?

Once you buy a share of REIT, you own a physical asset that has a long-expected life span and there is a lot of potential to generate income through renting and property appreciation. Not only will you have the ownership rights of a property, you can also participate in the income generated by the property. This creates a sense of security for the investors as you will have a right over your property as well as enjoy the benefits of your income.

Another distinct advantage of buying a REIT is that you can invest without having to put in large amounts of capital or labor. Moreover, as more and more funds are put together in your real estate pool, you can create a greater amount of diversification in your portfolio and buy numerous properties. This is a great way to reduce the problems associated with buying a single asset.

You can imagine it might not be very easy to buy and maintain many investment properties on your own. You would have to put in a substantial amount of time and money in an investment which is not easily liquidated.

On the other hand, if you buy a Real Estate Investment Trust, your capital investment is limited to the price of your unit. The amount of labor you must put in is equal to the amount of research that is required and lastly, your shares are liquid on regular stock exchanges.

Another thing you need to know is that REITs must distribute nearly 90% of their yearly taxable income, i.e. income produced by real estate to their shareholders. The final and perhaps the most important advantage of buying a REIT is that you will earn a lot of profit as the holder of a REIT.

Also, higher rate of distribution means that you have more chances of making excess cash on your investment. This feature distinguishes REITs from other investments such as common stocks where the company's board of directors decides whether extra cash should be distributed to the common stockholder.

How You Can Pick the Right REIT

Like other types of investments, you need to do your homework before deciding which REIT is right for you. Here are some simple tips that will help you with your decision.

1. Understand the track record of the managers and their team.

Before you jump into buying the first portion of managed real estate pool you come across, take some time to understand and evaluate the track record of a company's manager and team.

Remember, profits you earn after buying a REIT are closely related to the manager's ability to identify and pick the right investments. The manager also needs to decide upon the best strategy when choosing the best investment.

2. Have a close look at the diversification of your portfolio.

As mentioned earlier, Real Estate Investment Trusts are more focused on the ownership of property and the real estate market is influenced by location and type of property.

If you decide to buy a REIT, it is crucial that you buy a share only when your desired portfolio is diversified. If your Real Estate Investment Trust is dominated by commercial real estate, you might face problems in the future if there is a drop in occupancy rates.

Your REIT also needs to have enough capital to fund future growth initiatives and maintain a diversified portfolio for increased returns.

3. The numbers count!

One final thing that you should keep in mind before buying a specific REIT is its earnings, i.e. funds created from operations and, of course cash that is available for distribution.

Remember, these numbers are very important as they measure the overall performance of the Real Estate Investment Trust and determine the money that will be distributed to you as an investor.

Be careful to not focus only on the numbers generated by the REIT. Remember, the final numbers are only useful if you've looked closely at the other two signs, diversification and the role of management. This is because the money you make is influenced by the diversification of your portfolio as well as the management's choice in picking real estate investments.

The bottom line is that there are a lot of different ways to invest money and increase wealth and this applies to stocks, REITs, bonds, mutual funds, DRIPs and any other investment. With all important decisions, it is crucial that you think clearly and then make a well-informed decision. Having said this, REITs also have a great deal of interesting features that make them a good fit in your investment portfolio.

REITs in the United States

REITs are companies that own and operate "income producing" real estate. You will also come across some Real Estate Investment Trusts that finance real estate. To qualify as a REIT in the United States, a company must distribute at least 90% of its taxable income to its shareholders in the form of dividends annually. Moreover, under U.S. tax rules, a REIT company must:

1. Have a corporation, trust, or association structure

2. Have a board of directors or trustees to manage the company

3. Have more than 75% of total assets invested in real estate

4. Have valid transferable shares or transferable certificates of interest

5. Have 100 persons or more as joint owners

6. Not be a financial institution or an insurance company

7. Distribute 90% of its taxable income to its shareholders

8. Have 95% of its income as a result of interest and property income. Moreover, 75% of the company's gross income should come from rents or mortgage interest.

Chapter 23 Minimum Reasonable Expectation

Fantasy sports may, indeed, be games of skill, but there is an undeniable level of 'luck' at play. Small or large, it is a non-zero factor. Unfortunately, our own efforts cannot influence said luck – 'freak accidents' are, by definition, irregular and, thus, unpredictable – but we can somewhat decrease the factor by which luck impacts our fantasy team.

We will start with a few assumptions that must be accepted. With further research, they can probably be refuted. We don't want that. We want a conservative approach, and each of the axioms are built to achieve the goal of limiting 'dangerous' exposure.

Injuries will happen and, while we cannot pinpoint the aforementioned 'freak accident,' we can build in some cushion for those players who have had a history of missing time due to chronic ailments. If we can buy into a player that can only give us 100 games, then we would be pleasantly surprised if he delivered a full season. We will gladly welcome the additional contribution.

Many projection systems consider an average of production over a specific set of time. Averages could be extremely misleading. If Player A hits 15 home runs for three consecutive seasons, and Player B had seasons of 5, 15, and 25 home runs, respectively, they both produce the same average of 15 home-runs-per-season. If we value consistency higher than upside, we would be targeting Player A. If we can target high risk-reward hitters, Player B is more appealing. Whatever the preferred plan-of-attack, don't take averages at face value.

For the sake of discussion, rumors about shifting the batting order hold little value until the player moves within the lineup. Don't buy in until you see it. Assume that said hitter will bat in a position no better than where he finished last season.

By now, it should be evident what we are trying to accomplish. We are creating a set of 'worst-case scenarios' that can be applied to our players and their respective projections.

With some governing rules established, we can condense them into a somewhat tangible variable. This yields the player's baseline. It is the minimum reasonable expectation. MRE, if you will. And, it has its own slogan that reads, "When in doubt, round down."

This is far from the first or last place where you will come across the desire to approximate a player's baseline — it is one of the most common practices in statistical analysis of fantasy sports — but it is worth highlighting when to use it and how much weight we assign to it and its components. As is the case with nearly everything in this world, proceeding on a case-by-case basis is preferred, where possible. If we can't, we will note the exceptions and where and why we adjusted as we did.

Returning to the axiom and example about averages, we can determine that, while Player A exhibited impressive consistency over a three-year period, Player B is the one we want to consider for our fantasy team. But only if we use the correct number. That is, his minimum output of five home runs.

If we base this player's projections on the worst production he has had, we will pay a lower price and, thus, take a smaller risk. Then again, if we are too conservative, we will almost certainly miss out on said player altogether, especially if he most recently delivered 25 home runs and is showing the makings of a potential 'breakout candidate.' How do we balance this?

We already accepted that risk is part of the game. Somewhere, we will have to take chances. Just not when the talent levels are thin.

Prior to the 2016 season, there was a debate within fantasy baseball circles as to whether Mike Trout or Bryce Harper deserved to be taken with the first overall pick. Quite frankly, this argument was silly. Trout had established himself as one of the best hitters in baseball over his previous four seasons, three of which featured no fewer than 157 games. Harper exploded in 2015 as the National League Most Valuable Player and deserved nothing but praise for his extraordinary performance. However, it was, indeed, extraordinary.

Over Harper's previous three seasons – one of which was his rookie campaign, he played an average of 119 games-per-year. The worst indictment of this statistic is that his rookie year – 139 games played – was the season in which he played the most games – contrary to the typical career path, where a player would ease his way into the league. In fact, 139 games decreased to 118 games in 2013, then 100 games in 2014.

When given a nearly full workload of 153 games, Harper delivered in a big way. In fact, if we focus on Harper's output-per-at-bat – a key metric – it was easy to project another stellar year, if he remained on the field.

Sometimes, it is that simple.

If Bryce Harper remained on the baseball field – i.e. not injured – he would deliver high returns. But what had led anybody to believe that he would repeat 153 games when he was already two full seasons removed from his previous high of 139?

Absolutely nothing.

The writing was on the wall that, indeed, he could repeat his performance, but it was more likely that he wouldn't be given the opportunity to do so. Harper ultimately played in 147 games – a surprisingly high number, given the history – but was a far cry from the 'best player in baseball.' His numbers took a dramatic dive in the categories of runs scored, runs batted in, hits, doubles, and, most noticeably, home runs and batting average. Not only did he miss some time, but he appeared to be playing through injuries that didn't quite force him out of the lineup and resulted in a catastrophically bad return on investment.

Despite his upside, taking Bryce Harper with one of the top few picks in 2016 was simply not worth the risk. Harper was not necessarily the only player to disappoint – Clayton Kershaw and Paul Goldschmidt come to mind – but he should have been the least surprising compared to his average draft position. And, if a fantasy owner actively decided to select Harper over Trout, he or she was certainly burned as Trout put together another MVP campaign.

The analogy between Players A and B concludes with the difference between consistency and upside relative to risk. In the first round – in the case of Trout and Harper, the first two picks of a draft – we want consistent excellence. We want Trout. In the later rounds, we want to pay for Player B's upside at his lowest price. We want Harper at a discount.

Thankfully, there are always an abundance of players whose minimum baseline is within reasonable expectations. Sprinkle in upside and we have our first set of 'sleepers.' Most are 'rebound candidates.' Here are a few for the 2017 season:

Jose Bautista – A consensus early-round pick for the last half-dozen years, Bautista's explosion into the upper echelon of fantasy hitters finally fizzled. It did not, however, completely diminish. The Blue Jays' slugger – who just had his streak of six consecutive years with an All-Star appearance snapped – saw virtually every one of his important statistics suffer in a 'walk year' in 2016, but he gets a mulligan in '17 with basically another one-year contract. With 2014-2016 featuring home run totals of 35, 40, and 22, respectively, we can find immense room for growth if we pay the price for 22 home runs – a later round, since Bautista's stock has plummeted – and receive anything more by season's end.

Dallas Keuchel – The write-up on Jose Bautista should act as the template for most of this group, as evidenced by sliding seamlessly into a breakdown of Dallas Keuchel. His last three seasons' earned run averages are 2.93, 2.48, and 4.55. Granted, Keuchel doesn't have the longevity in his resume as Bautista, but the Astros' 'ace' pitcher is only one season removed from winning the Cy Young award. Most importantly, Keuchel did not concede every category in his 'down' year, as he was still an excellent source of strikeouts-per-inning-pitched. With one statistic stabilized, the rest can follow.

Felix Hernandez – A third 'rebound candidate,' Felix Hernandez is arguably the most consistently great player of the group. He has the long-term track record of success that dwarfs that of Keuchel, while also winning the developmental race to stardom – Bautista was a non-factor for the first six years of his career, while Hernandez continually blossomed as expected. The knock on the Mariners' 'ace' is that he has now delivered two consecutive underwhelming seasons, but it would be naïve to ignore his previous seven years, during which he finished in the top-four of Cy Young voting four times – winning once.

Miguel Sano – A 'sleeper' of a different sort, Miguel Sano's downward spiral does not stem from previous success that has failed to be repeated. It stems from simply missing expectations. Sano's calling card is power and, while he certainly can launch nearly any pitch over the fence, his 25 home runs in 2016 are easy to lose in the shuffle. What Sano does have in his favor is the pedigree of a once-top-prospect now entering his third season. It is extremely plausible that another offseason of work will benefit Sano drastically, and we would be barely risking more than a bench spot to secure his incredibly high ceiling.

Brian McCann – After playing in Yankee Stadium – a left-handed power hitter's dream venue – it seemed impossible for Brian McCann to land in an equally-desirable situation. Perhaps his new ballpark isn't as ideal as his old one, but Brian McCann shifting to the deep lineup of Houston is a fair tradeoff. At a position that remains relatively scarce – of course, after the top players – McCann will likely see an increase in opportunities to drive in runs, maintain his power output, and still reap the rewards of playing in the American League by serving as the team's designated hitter when he is not catching.

Anthony Rendon – The story of Anthony Rendon never changes. He holds incredible upside, but simply cannot stay on the field long enough to reach it. At least, not consistently. Thankfully, alternating years of full-length and shortened campaigns help further the perception that Rendon "never" stays healthy. It isn't true, and his 156 games in 2016 marked the second time in three years that he reached the 150-game barrier. Rendon does suffer slightly from losing his eligibility at second base, but otherwise is an overlooked asset in a deep lineup.

Raja Davis – The speedster may have made it into the introduction of this book thanks to his power heroics in the World Series for the Cleveland Indians, but Raja Davis now has a new home atop the Athletics' lineup. By virtue of shifting from the American League champions to an Oakland organization that has struggled in recent years, Davis is suddenly a forgotten talent. It would be wise to remember that he has stolen at least 34 bases in seven-of-his-last-eight seasons and can be acquired at an incredibly low price.

Michael Brantley – The opening to this chapter creates the ideal bookend for the finale where we can, again, assess a level of risk we are willing to take based on an expected price tag. Let's ask ourselves a pair of questions. If Michael Brantley plays a full season, can he produce early round value? Absolutely. But, will he play a full season of Major League Baseball? According to his track record, it is unlikely. Attempting to project the amount of games Brantley plays might truly be riskier than drafting him altogether, but we can use our simple rule as a protective measure: round down. Whatever contributions we project from Brantley, we can conservatively slash them. We know how high his potential is but reaching it would be nothing more than icing on an inexpensive – but good – cake.

Chapter 24 Why do companies paying a growing dividend have excellent stock market performance?

A regularly increasing dividend over a long period is proof that the company has a competitive advantage. Without this advantage, it could not steadily increase its distributable profits whatever the economic situation and the pressure of competition. It also proves that the company's profitability is solid and not at all related to the fleeting effects of a favorable conjecture. The logic of a profitable business is the following. The steady increase in profit leads to the increase of the dividend. The dividend growth year after year shows that the company manages to increase its profits. The regularity of these payments shows a management of quality and a policy favorable to the shareholders.

The constant payment of a dividend and its systematic increase is appreciated by the financial markets. Indeed, the investor does not have to wait to sell his shares to cash his first profits. This significantly reduces the risk he takes to own a title. Since there is no need to sell, the shares of this type of company are less volatile. In addition, the steady growth of the dividend also puts the investor in a position to be able to receive a supplement of income immune from monetary erosion. It is protected against the loss of purchasing power of long-term inflation. The steady growth of the dividend thus ends up leading to an increase in the stock market valuation of the company. For example, if in a few years a company can double its dividend, then the share price will also double. It's not magic but it's mathematical:

growing profit + increasing dividend = long-term share price rise

The valuation of the company on the stock market reflects not only the value of its assets but also its ability to generate money. In terms of "stock market performance", companies that distribute increasing dividends are beating their benchmark which is, let us remember, the average performance of the market. Conversely, in the case of companies that pay a stagnant dividend, decrease it, or worse, cut it, the performance is lower than the same index.

For the long-term shareholder, the profit is double. Not only does he receive a growing dividend but, in addition, he sees the value of his investment in the listed company increase over the years. It is for this reason that many investors are seeking on the financial market's companies paying a growing dividend. These are victims of the demand and see their price reach high valuations. Companies that pay stagnant, declining or cutting dividends should be considered harmful to the long-term investor. They are to deviate from his stock market.

KEY POINTS
1) A listed company that generates increasing revenues and increasing dividends sees its stock market value grow over time.

2) An investor with a growing dividend-paying company is getting doubly rich: with the increase in dividends and the value of the share price.

3) Companies paying increasing dividends are high-quality companies that are highly sought after by investors, which leads to a high valuation of their share price.

Chapter 25 Key Elements That Define Insider and Outsider Group Membership

We can all relate in some way to insider–outsider dynamics because we've all had at least some experience as both insiders and outsiders. Even those of us with many insider group memberships— including the authors, who are white, male, upper middle class, not living with a disability, and in possession of master's degrees—have some outsider group membership. For example, one of us is Jewish and one of us grew up working class. Some of these insider-outsider groups are fixed and global, such as gender. Across the world, men almost uniformly have the insider status based on their gender, and women have outsider group status. Some will change as context changes, such as age. In much of the West older age is associated with a decline and less ability to learn, while in parts of Asia older people are held in great esteem, as wise. As we describe the core insider– outsider dynamics below, think of your own collection of insider and outsider group memberships.

Level of Awareness

When we are in an outsider group, we are much more likely to be aware of the difference, aware of our group membership. Think about how much left-handers know about handedness. Why is this? It is because barriers often emerge that are based on the group membership. If I, as a right-hander, am not aware of those barriers, how can I anticipate or adjust to minimize them? When we are in the insider group, "ignorance is bliss." Why would a person need to be aware of a group membership that isn't causing a barrier or a problem?

Ask an LGBT (lesbian, gay, bisexual, or transgender) person who works for a company, "What is it like to be LGBT in this company?" and you will likely have a rich conversation about managing personal identity at work, deciding what to tell coworkers about your life outside of work, and balancing openness against potential risks. Ask a heterosexual person, "What is it like to be heterosexual in this company?" and you will probably get a blank stare. This is not a criticism of heterosexuals. If you are heterosexual, there's no need to think about your identity because it is the norm. On Monday morning, when asked what you did over the weekend, you reply, "My husband (or wife) and I found a great new restaurant in Brooklyn." Does it occur to you that you just came out? Probably not.

If you are white and in a large corporate meeting, do you notice that out of the two hundred people in the room there are only two who appear to be persons of color? Probably not. Does your African American colleague notice? There is a good chance he notices almost immediately. It is most likely your differently abled colleagues are very aware of the accessibility of the building because they need to plan for access with their wheelchairs. Your Indian colleague who works remotely likely notices how few of his comments get acknowledged and built on in team meetings. If you are his white or US-born colleague you probably haven't noticed that, at least as a pattern. Our different levels of awareness have huge implications for forging a path toward greater inclusion.

Different Pattern of Experience

Being an insider or outsider produces a fundamentally different pattern of experience. Insider group membership generally creates a positive pattern of experience. For example, insiders are generally seen as the norm, given the benefit of the doubt, and assumed to deserve the position of leadership they have attained. Nothing bad is likely to happen based on their insider group status. This is a group-level statement: something "bad" can happen to any individual at any time. What we are talking about here is "good" or "bad" happening to us based on our group membership, not our individuality. We are also talking well beyond the random events than can befall any of us. We are talking instead about patterns.

Think about a woman executive. It is possible that on any given day all the following things could happen:

• On her walk into work, she gets whistled at by a group of men who call her "baby."

- Standing near a desk in the reception area of her office, she is assumed to be a secretary or receptionist by a visitor.

- She attends several meetings at which she is the only woman.

- When calling on a client, she is assumed to be subordinate to the male staff member accompanying her to the meeting.

- She gets feedback from her boss that she is being a little too aggressive and it is causing some of her male peers to not want to collaborate with her.

- She observes four of her male peers setting a date for a golf outing.

Most of these events could happen to a male executive, but it is highly unlikely this would be a pattern of experience for a male executive. These patterns fundamentally shape our experiences and our perceptions. We have seen the prevalence of harassment in the last couple of years as the #MeToo movement, a movement in which women (for the most part) publicly announced their workplace sexual harassment experiences, brought great awareness to the vastly different experiences of men and women. How many men, like us, were shocked and saddened at the numbers of women who tweeted or posted #MeToo on their social media feeds. As insiders, we see these things as unfortunate, isolated instances, occasional annoyances that can be brushed off easily rather than as situations that need to be addressed as conditions that affect the business in a serious way. As outsiders, we see this pattern of experiences as overtly hostile or, at a minimum, as one that saps our energy and productivity, creating barriers to a successful career.

Willingness to Engage

Outsiders and insiders are often reluctant to engage about their group membership, but for different reasons. Insiders can find it hard to talk about the impact of something they are not even aware of. Also, there can be a sense that there is nothing worth talking about when it comes to their group identity. Why would I want to talk about what it means to be white, male, or upper middle class? These attributes do not seem like a valuable or relevant conversation starter. In the United States there is a value that says we are not supposed to see ourselves as groups. Instead, we are encouraged to see ourselves as fully empowered individuals, in control of our own destiny. We should ignore our group memberships whenever possible, is the implicit message.

For outsiders, the reluctance is mostly based on two things. One is internal: there is a reluctance to acknowledge and focus on barriers outsiders feel they have little control over. To talk about the impact of being LGBT, for example, can be upsetting and demoralizing. The other factor is external, and is at play especially when the conversation is with a member of the insider group: How will the other person react to what I have to say? Will he believe me? Will she think I am talking about her and her behavior, and thus get defensive? Will he try to explain away what I am saying, by saying, "Oh, that's happened to me too, don't worry about it." Will I be perceived as a victim? Is it worth investing the energy in this conversation and would anything be likely to change because of it?

All too often, the conversation is not explored in the beginning because of reluctance on both sides. In Sarah's story, from our earlier example, failing to have the conversation ends up with a separation. At any point before Sarah made her decision to leave, a member of the insider group would have had the most impact if he were attuned to Sarah feeling like an outsider. Sarah really wanted to fit in and succeed at her new firm. She was already visibly different from the group. If she called attention to the atmosphere, it would only make her appear more like an outsider. Once Sarah made the decision to leave, she felt there was no reason to, and most likely had no energy to, open the discussion. Her explanation simply fed into the vicious cycle of preconceived biases, making it harder for the next woman.

Setting Norms Versus Adapting to Norms

Being in an outsider group generally means having to understand and adjust to the insider group's ways of thinking and doing. Much of the experience of left-handers, in terms of their handedness, is about adjusting or adapting to a right-handed world. This norm extends to all, or at least most, group memberships. For example, most women in managerial positions must adapt to a male-dominated culture. This means adapting to a business culture that is normed around male behavior and preferences. How to compete, how to network, how to distinguish yourself, how to engage others, how to disagree or agree—in most businesses, these are built around male-socialized norms. This doesn't mean women can't succeed but it does mean, all too often, that success is somewhat dependent upon women's ability to adapt and assimilate to the other gender's norms.

Think about the leadership style that is viewed most positively in your office culture. There is a good chance it is normed around male-socialized leadership behavior. There is also a good chance that, culturally, it is US or Western-based. The norm likely is visible, extroverted, and very assertive people. We see a pattern in many companies in which Asians get to the highest technical jobs, but much less often get promoted into leadership and management positions. We think this is at least partially due to the fact many Asians are acculturated into a more subtle and quiet form of leadership, which doesn't fit the leadership profile popular in many Western-based organizations.

Obviously, there are many outsider group members, be they women, LGBT folks, ethnic minorities, etc., who successfully adapt and assimilate. What is the cost of depending upon exceptional individuals to adapt and change much of who they are in order to succeed? What is lost in translation? What is the impact on others, who are quite capable and skilled, but are not able to assimilate quite enough? Are the benefits of diversity in innovation realized when individuals feel like they need to conform to the status quo? Alternatively, can a polyculture environment be as productive as a culture where everyone fits a norm?

Implications of Insider–Outsider Dynamics

Progress toward a more level playing field and efforts to create more inclusive organizations are difficult and take time. This is true whether we are speaking of organizational change efforts or about societal change. Think about how long it took to achieve certain milestones of legal equality in the United States and any number of other countries for any number of groups. Think about how much resistance there was and how much upheaval followed. We believe insider–outsider dynamics are at the heart of this challenge.

The fundamental challenge right from the start is that outsider groups have more information about the dynamics and less power to change them. Insiders have less information and more power. This creates an obvious barrier to change. If there is no "burning platform" for insiders, then why would they do anything?

The problem with putting out a set of challenges very directly is that it can be risky; it's what some of our colleagues call a "career-limiting move." Outsiders feel reluctant to share their perspectives because they might be perceived as whining and complaining and focusing on the negative, and because these views can create defensiveness among insiders. Insiders almost always have more power in the hierarchy, which only exacerbates the challenge.

To the extent outsiders don't share their true experiences, the less-informed insider perspective rules the day. Insiders' perceptions are reinforced, the perspective doesn't change, behavior doesn't shift, and insider–outsider dynamics continue. This serves to reinforce outsiders' perception that it is too risky or even useless, to honestly and clearly share their perspectives and experiences. They, and we, become stuck.

Often, this leads to adaptation and more assimilation. Some outsiders are better at this than others, and they succeed. Insiders see this as proof that anyone can make it and the playing field is open and level. Are you getting a sense for why this kind of change is hard? We call this the cycle of the status quo.

Cycle of Status Quo

How do we break this cycle and move ahead in a quicker, more powerful way? The good news is that this cycle can be broken at any point.

At steps one and two, for example, what would happen if a change agent inside an organization decided to tap the perspectives of outsider group members? What if the effort was set up in a way that was anonymous enough to reduce the perception of risk? What if this effort was led by an insider, so the power was used not to unintentionally suppress outsiders' perspectives, but instead to fully understand the perspective? Perhaps it would be even more powerful if insiders' perspectives were sought as well. This would allow for comparison of the different information held by both groups. Would it be useful, for example, to get women's perspective on the impact of gender in an organization? We hope you are thinking, "Yes." Would it also be helpful to get men's perspective? We hope you still say, "Yes."

Unfortunately, many organizations ask about the perspectives of outsiders but forget to ask the insiders. In an odd way, this slows the change process. We told you outsiders have more information about what inclusion and exclusion look like in the organization, but it does not mean that insiders know nothing. Everyone's perspective is valuable in a long-term change effort. It is critical to engage both outsiders and insiders when the goal is creating sustainable inclusion. Organizations require all perspectives in order to forge a path forward. It is the gap between what outsiders know and what insiders know that can build the "creative tension," as Peter Senge would say, to move change along.

It is also important, referring to step two, to address the inherent power dynamic. Having a member of the insider group in charge of the change effort can neutralize the power dynamic to some extent and help the organization to get the information that will allow for an effective change strategy. We observe many D&I efforts led by individuals who have visible or important outsider group memberships. Their perspective as outsiders is very important in creating a change strategy—but if they are the only visible change agent, the impact may be diminished because they won't be representing the insider's perspective. We strongly recommend inclusion change efforts include insider group members in visible leadership positions, if not as the head of D&I, then at least as a visible sponsor. This is a strong symbol that tells insiders they shouldn't write off the inclusion effort as intended to make members of the outsider group happier or more satisfied at work. In this insider-involved scenario, a business case can emerge, a burning platform from which to launch real change. Most successful organizations know how to drive change once they have determined it is important to their success and survival.

During the writing of this book's first edition, a presidential election was taking place. One of the major issues was the right of women to choose medical procedures for their own bodies. Historically, political campaign advertisements on this issue featured women. Because most politicians making the laws are men, women are the outsider group and men are firmly in the insider position. The advertisements featuring women were somewhat helpful in changing female voting tendencies, however, they did not have a measurable impact on men. One of the New Hampshire gubernatorial candidates realized it would be more powerful if men, the insider group, advocated positions on women's issues. Using this approach, the campaign was able to move the needle not only with women but also with men. The message suddenly had a more powerful reach.

Once groundwork is laid, step four must be addressed in a straightforward manner. Insider group members must learn about the difference, and they must have a way to think about it more fully. They need to know about the business impact of exclusion. Because most of them are well intentioned, they need to understand they are not being indicted as bad people. When it comes to this kind of awareness education, we take a strong stance that exclusion or bias is often unintentional, and inclusion needs to be intentional. Most managers intend to be inclusive, so it can be helpful for them to see how their positive intent does not automatically translate to an inclusive outcome.

Ultimately, the most powerful change occurs when both insiders and outsiders are fully engaged. For insiders, this often involves finding our own self-interest. We know this sounds rather self-serving. However, human beings tend to do things that are consistent with their own interests. If I, as an insider, see inclusion as only about helping disadvantaged groups, I may well act out of a moral imperative or a sense of obligation, but my motivation is increased when I also see how I will benefit.

As insiders, we benefit in direct and indirect ways from the inclusion of outsiders. When the Americans with Disabilities Act passed the US Congress in 1991, certainly some people living with disabilities benefited substantially via access to buildings and public spaces. But how many of us not living with a physical disability also benefited when we could more easily ride our bikes with the cut curbs? How many times have you rolled a suitcase up a ramp instead of trying to drag it upstairs? How many times have you used automatic doors when your hands were full? Do we not all benefit when our teams are stronger because we have broader inclusion? Do our decisions improve because of a more engaged, diverse group of colleagues?

Chapter 26 Dividend Growth Stock Suggestions to Start Your Portfolio

So far, we have explained the benefits of investing in dividend stocks, the type of long-term strategies to consider when making those decisions, as well as how to notice the warning signs when looking at the plethora of options through a variety of sectors and options. So, which are the best ones to consider?

1. Large-Cap

As it has been mentioned several times, there are a lot of large corporations that have established themselves as dependable choices that investors have counted on for their long-term investment strategies.

Name brands like Coca-Cola, Walmart, McDonald's and the like won't provide the biggest jumps in their dividend payments, if they do at all. There's unlikely to be any large increase of distributed dividends for the shareholders because it has grown so much by becoming a global brand. What is likely to happen is that you will see steady growth as more people become attached to a company.

This isn't a bad sign because there are plenty of large-cap dividend growth stocks that have a long history of increasing the amount of money that they pay their investors– please refer to the S&P 500's "Dividend Aristocrats."

2. Small-Cap

On the flip side, some investors may not want to put all their money into large corporations. Maybe they want to put some money into smaller companies that have not only shown potential growth, but are within an industry sector (which we will list a few later on in this chapter) that has opportunities to grow even more because of consumer demand and other factors.

That doesn't mean you should consider putting a lot of your money into too many of these smaller companies 1) because you want a diverse portfolio and 2) not all small companies are going to rise like the bigger corporations have in the past. There is a little more risk with that potential for a higher reward.

3. Real Estate

It's no secret that the housing market has seen some declines with homeowners finding themselves under water in their home loans. But the market is cyclical in many ways, meaning that there will always been ebbs and flows that are like a roller coaster – the real estate economy is currently at one of its all-time lows.

But this shouldn't last long as there are several real estate experts who are predicting that there will be a giant boom as the demand for new homes continues to grow and the population growing in the United States. Now would be a perfect time to invest when the shares are low and should see some growth eventually. It's a matter of when, not if.

4. Technology Corporations

Sure, we aren't at the point that the older 1960s and 1970s cartoons like the Jetsons predicted we would find ourselves at by now – flying cars, homes in the sky, and food that comes in pill form. But every day there is something new to keep an eye out for – the most recent example was the new smart watch where people can do everything from calling someone to checking emails on their wrist.

It's evolving and investors can put their money into new products and the companies that develop them. You may consider adding some that offer dividend distribution payments, including a few technology start-ups into your portfolio. You never know what the next big thing could be – just imagine if you were one of the early investors in Microsoft or Apple.

5. Telecommunications

Everyone has a cell phone or a mobile device that can act like one to connect them to anyone around the world and a big part of that is the evolving World Wide Web. While most people are already connected in the U.S. and neighboring countries, there is a growing demand that companies here are starting to notice overseas.

The markets in Africa and the Middle East have some of the largest demands that are increasing by the day and attracting attention from businesses like Amazon. Consider companies in that field a safe bet with a few more possible booms as use of the internet and the need for connection and security continue to evolve.

6. Financial Market

There are a number of banks and credit cards that are getting some attention – including U.S. Bank, which according to a story from The Street, is seeing revenue increases that have risen above the industry average by nearly 1 percent. Sure, it seems minor, but it's a step in the right direction.

The same goes from other banking institutions like Wells Fargo and Chase, which continue to be solid investment options because the potential need for homes (as references above in "real estate") will require a need for things like home loans. The growing population will also mean that in another 10 to 20 years, there will be a new generation of drivers in need of auto loans to drive to school and work. Speaking of which ....

7. Automotive

There's a reason that The Street put General Motors at the top of their list of the top 10 dividend-paying stocks – based on what big-time investor Warren Buffet has done with his portfolio. More cars are always being produced and being sought after by a variety of consumers and have their own desires that range from an economic fuel rating to the color of the paint used.

Regarding GM, they have a current yield of about 4 percent and should maintain that level, if not increase annually, without too much of a problem. The net income has more than tripled in the past year, according to The Street. Additionally, public transportation also falls under automotive in a way because many of these companies continue to help produce buses, taxi cabs and limousines.

8. Alternative Fuels

Well, something must power all these vehicles on the road. While there is so much focus on using electricity to power them, there is also a demand for more green-friendly ways to replace gasoline and diesel options like ethanol, biodiesel, natural gas, propane and hydrogen.

Expect some big returns as these options become more available to the public and the automotive industry continues to make vehicles that run on these types of alternative fuels. If you include some of these stocks in your portfolio, you will be thinking green for the planet's environment as well as your wallet.

9. Restaurants - Dining

The people of the world need to eat but having a few restaurant stocks should be done in a way that adds some beneficial diversity to your dividend investment portfolio. The reason this has made the list because there is a growing community among social media outlets where people have gained a fascination with the food that they eat and comment on where they got it – Twitter, Instagram, Facebook and Foursquare.

YouTube is also becoming a popular place to find honest food reviewers. When people here several of these video uploaders – and some have hundreds of thousands of subscribers – more people will want to go to that restaurant to try the newest concoction of meat, cheese and bacon (yes, bacon is still growing and if it could be a stock, you should go for that as well).

And as more diners and eating establishments continue to create larger meals for those who look for a dietary challenge, there is a population of eaters who will try and are willing to spend up to $40-50 to do so.

Chapter 27 How Pick a technically and Fundamentally Stock for Dividend Portfolio

When an investor decides to buy a dividend stock, he should look at several different aspects. In the discussion above, we have explicitly discussed various factors for dividend investing and we have also outlined fundamental and technical aspects of dividend investing.

Let's draw two examples. In the first case will discuss why Caterpillar is a solid pick for dividend investors, while the second case will also discuss why General Electric is a poor buy for dividend investors.

Caterpillar Is Great Dividend Stock, But Wait for Buying Opportunity

Caterpillar is among those companies that have extensive dividend history and large business models. Their revenue and cash generation potential are also strong enough to support dividends. In addition, its payout ratio is standing in the range of 30 to 40% of income, which is considered as perfect payout ratio for dividend investors.

Therefore, investors can pick Caterpillar for their dividend stock portfolio. But it's also important for investors to choose the right time for entering the company. If an investor buys a stock at 52-weeks high, this is couldn't help him in generating higher gains from share price appreciation, but he would be entitled to get big dividends.

The company's share price declined sharply in the second half of 2015 and hit the bottom in the beginning of 2016. Let do fundamental analysis of why its share price dipped sharply and how it again got a boom after few months.

Buying companies on the dip with strong future fundamentals is always deemed as a perfect trading strategy. Caterpillar is among those companies that have strong market presence in global markets and its brand recognition and technological innovations continue to help it in extending the market share.

Its share price started plunging in late 2015 due to the depression in the basic material sectors. It has been receiving the largest portion of revenue from the basic material sector. Lower commodity prices of mining products and the volatility in oil prices forced mining and energy companies to decline their investments, which eventually impacted demand for CAT's products.

However, wise investors know that commodity prices are cyclical in nature and they have the potential to make strong bounce backs. CAT's stock price hit the lowest level of $59 a share in the beginning of 2016. That was the perfect time for dividends to jump into this company. Its share price movement on the candlestick chart also presented strong Bullish Engulfing Candlestick pattern when it hit $59 a share. However, CAT's stock has also presented Bullish Engulfing Candlestick pattern in the next quarters, which was the indication of the longer uptrend in the price movement.

However, its stock isn't a perfect buy now. It is currently trading at the highest level in its history. Moreover, overvalued valuations are also making it a pricey pick. Its share price is currently hovering close to 90 times to earnings, compared to the industry average of 30 times. Although, the stock is unlikely to make a massive downturn due to strong financial outlook, investors should look for bearish Engulfing

Candlestick pattern to appear before buying this quality dividend stock.

Why General Electric Isn't a Buy for Dividend Investors?

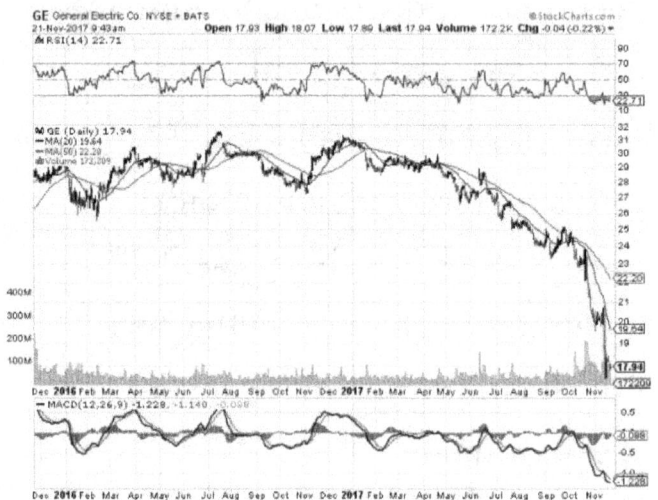

The dip in share price is always not a buying opportunity. In addition, strong future fundamentals are very important for the stock to keep the uptrend. General Electric has presented two perfect examples for dividend investors. Its stock price increased steadily in 2016, as the company started restructuring its business model and the management has presented a rosy picture for the future.

However, advanced investors with a strong understanding of industrial businesses knew that the company would take longer time in moving back their business model to industrial business from financial services. Thus, they were expecting its share price to plunge but investors with less understanding of future fundamentals were easily fooled by the rosy presentations from the management.

With the beginning of 2017, investors started realizing that the restructuring process will take a longer time and the company needs massive cash inflows to support the change. Thus, its share price started declining. But the dip in its share price wasn't the perfect buying opportunity, as its cash flow position and lower earning potential were creating difficulties for the company to sustain its dividend. Therefore, recently the company announced to slash its dividend by 50%.

Candlestick chart patterns and moving averages were also presenting the downward trend in its share price since the start of this year. There was more than one bearish Engulfing Candlestick pattern appeared on its chart in the last eleven months. GE isn't presenting a buying opportunity despite the massive selloff. The company's future fundamentals are bleak and cash position isn't strong enough to support dividends and restructuring actions. The company needs to make several acquisitions in the days to come to expand its presence in the industrial businesses.

Chapter 28 Having the compound interest force on your side!

There are two types of interest: simple interest and compound interest. Simple interest is calculated solely on capital. For example, if you invest in an asset with a simple interest rate of 5% (for example a life insurance), each year you will earn 5% of $1000: $50 the year number 1, $50 the year number 2, $50 year number 3... On the contrary, compound interest is calculated on the capitalized interest, that is to say, on the generated interest that is added to the capital to produce new interests. If you use a compound interest rate of 10%, each year you earn 10% of the amount + the interest of the previous year. For instance, $1000 invested will produce $100 interest in the year number 1, $110 the year number 2 (10% x (1000 + 100), $121 the year number 3 (10% x (1100 + 110) ...

As you can see, in the long run, the difference is dizzying between simple interest and compound interest. The purpose of this chapter is to make you aware that you must start investing with compound interest now even if you start with little. Systematically reinvesting interest earned on your capital allows you to multiply it faster. Simple interests multiply initial capital in a linear (and therefore slow) way.

Another good news is that it is possible to accelerate the principle of compound interest by reinvesting its earnings at a faster rate (in the examples given above, the earnings were reinvested only once at the end of the year). If you buy shares which pay you a monthly dividend rather than an annual dividend (for example: Canadian / US REITs), you can reinvest the dividends every month, which will speed up the pace of wealth creation.

You can further accelerate the process by playing two tables at once: the strength of compound interest (by not affecting your capital and reinvesting your dividends at a monthly rate) and an interest rate that increases from year to year thanks to increasing dividend stocks. You will then benefit from a "double composition" of interests. It's interesting to note that companies like Coca-Cola have been raising dividends every year for 53 years and Wal-Mart has been doing so for 42 years!

Being paid more and more without doing anything will allow you to create cash flow automatically. You will have frequent cash flow (through dividends) that will allow you to greatly accelerate your enrichment speed. The snowball effect here is very strong since three factors are playing in your favor simultaneously: the increase in the dividend paid, the strength of compound interest and the increase in the price of securities. What else do you want?

KEY POINTS
1) Compound interest produces more wealth than simple interest in the long term.
2) The investor has every interest not to be satisfied with receiving his increasing dividends. It must reinvest them in other

companies paying increasing dividends to
accelerate its enrichment.

BONUS! Day Trading Basics

It's time for you to look at the day trading process works. You could just blindly jump in, but that's a recipe for disaster. Instead, let's get you started on how to smartly engage in day trading.

The first question to ask yourself is how big an investment is you planning on making in your day trading efforts? You need to consider not only how much money you're willing to invest, but also how much time. Many investors look at day trading as an escape from their normal jobs, others see it as an answer to the uncertainties of the job market. While you may hunger to day trade full time, people do succeed as part time day traders while working a primary job. Beginners may also want to spend some time simulating investments to get a feel for how comfortable you are with the process and how much talent you may have. As mentioned in the last paragraph, simply jumping in is not a good idea. You need to understand the investment market, learn to look for indicators that give you an idea of stock movements, and make the most of your opportunities.

Infrastructure Concerns

While it may sound mundane, spending some time on your workspace and technology can be well worth it. Day trading can be stressful, so a work area that provides quiet and privacy can be helpful. Don't underestimate the importance of a reliable Internet connection and a backup method of controlling your investments in case your network goes down. These days it's not hard to have a fast land-based Internet connection while also having the ability to use your smartphone as a wireless hotspot if your main connection goes down. It only takes one network failure when you have a big investment on the line, to convince you of the importance of a backup Internet access plan.

Understanding the Market

It's one thing to say you want to invest in stocks. It's another thing to figure out what stocks you should be investing in. Investors break down the market into different sectors such as "retailers," "manufacturers," "utilities," "airlines," "energy," "health care," and others. Day traders can choose to target all these sectors or choose to specialize in one or more. As a beginner, focusing on one sector may be advantageous, particularly if it's one you're already familiar with.

Since as a day trader, you're interested in identifying opportunities for small, changes in stocks, not long-term growth. This means you'll need ample funding. U.S. based day traders need a minimum of $25,000 for their trading account, according to Securities and Exchange Commission (SEC) rules. This means you'd really need at least $30,000 to have some flexibility. Keep in mind; in the U.S. you can currently leverage your trading capital up to 400%. This means that you could control $120,000 worth of stock with your $30,000. As you learned earlier, this also means you could suffer four times the losses on your investments. Be aware too, that if you don't maintain your maintenance margin amount, you can receive a margin call. In planning for your trading account, it would be better to have more funds available, since that would make more stocks available for your consideration. Remember too, it's usually more cost efficient to buy shares in multiples of 100, meaning a small investment kitty will either limit you to cheaply priced stocks or buying stocks in smaller increments than are less cost effective. If you can devote more funds to your trading account, you'll be able to pursue more opportunities, and have the wherewithal to recover from losses.

Calculating a Simple Moving Average

The moving average is a basic tool investor use to monitor a stock's behavior over a defined period. The investor simply adds the stock's closing price for a specific period (two weeks, a month, a quarter, etc.) and then divides that number by the number of trading days in that period. A trader will calculate a short-term moving average and a long-term moving average for a stock (actually, you'll probably calculate a few more than this to get a better sense of the stock's behavior).

A simple moving average can tell you whether a stock is on a rising or declining trend.

An important point for many traders is when the short term moving average rises above or below the long-term moving average. A short-term moving average that crosses above a long-term moving average often indicates the stock is about to begin an upward trend. The opposite is also true.

One approach to using moving averages compares a specific short-term moving average (50 days) with a specific long-term moving average (200 days). If the 50-day average moves below the 200-day average, you have a bearish signal. This is known as a "Death Cross." If the 50 average moves above the 200-day average, it is a bullish signal, and is known as a "Golden Cross." While it would be nice if you could rely solely on such a simple system, remember that relying only on a moving average approach is unreliable. It's better to use this information as another bit of information when making your trading plans.

Choosing a Broker

Once you've decided on your trading allocation, you need to choose a broker or brokerage. There are several online discount brokers available to the novice investor. Many will offer you their own electronic trading program. Don't be surprised to get offers for free trades and a bonus for picking their firm. Free trades and cash bonuses are nice, but make sure you choose a broker you feel comfortable with and one that checks out with your research.

The biggest online brokerages include: TD Ameritrade, Scott Trade, Fidelity Brokerage, Charles Schwab, Options Express, Merrill Edge, Robinhood, Loyal3, Options House, Option, and others. Some like Robinhood offer free trades, making their overhead on charging interest on margin accounts and using customer cash to earn interest. Others may offer more services or access to more investment exchanges. One thing you won't get from any of these discount brokerages though is personal advice. That's the purview of the traditional broker.

In choosing a brokerage, consider the cost of trades, your comfort level with its trading program, and your ability to access the company's website. Also, investigate what others are saying about the brokerage and whether it handles the investment vehicles you're interested in trading.

Buy Orders, Sell Orders, and Setting a Stop Loss Price

Not every move a trader makes must be executed immediately or at random. You can tell your brokerage you only want to buy or sell a stock when it hits a certain price. The risk of course, is that the stock may not hit that price while you have money planned for it.

Chapter 29 You should also plan on setting a "Stop loss price," too. This is a protective move to make sure you don't get badly burned by the stock price moving in the wrong direction. Let's say you've bought shares of XYZ Corporation when their price was at $4.50 a share. Based on your research, you expect an upward move by the share price and plan on selling when it reaches $4.75 a share (always have an exit price planned). Then something goes wrong. Bad news upsets the market (in general or it effects your stock in particular), and your stock price starts dropping instead. Wisely, you left a stop loss order with your broker, in effect instructing the broker to automatically sell your shares when their price drops to a certain point (perhaps in this example $4.35) to limit your loss. You should know that stop loss orders aren't foolproof. Your broker still must find someone to buy the shares at that point. In times of crisis, share prices can fall so fast that they blow by the stop loss price and keep going before they finally sell, making your loss bigger than anticipated. While this isn't a regular occurrence, unexpected events can cause them. The company selling the Epi-pen recently saw its valuation drop $3 billion dollars in a short period of time because of news about its price markup. No day trader could have anticipated this news, and even with stop loss orders, traders who were expecting upward movement in this stock, probably lost more than they expected.

Chapter 30 Tip Checklist for the New ETF Investor

More investors who are looking to plan for their eventual retirement funds usually deal with a lot of concerns when it comes to selecting the right type of dividend-paying companies to include in their portfolio, and that requires having an idea of what to do and look out for.

Educate Yourself

Be prepared to do a lot of studying of the different sectors and the companies that they include—you'll want to have the proper knowledge to make your investment decisions.

Don't Try to Predict the Market

It's not something that can be done very easy, and even the best and most experienced investors know this. But a solid investment strategy will raise enough funds.

Some Stocks Have Red Flags

Some of the industries that have caused the most problems for investors include retail stores and the airline industry, which have seen the most volatile reactions in the market.

One Bad Apple Can Spoil the Whole Bunch

Therefore, investors need to keep an eye on all their stocks because one bad investment can reduce all the good that the rest of your portfolio has accumulated.

Don't Pay Too Much

While you want to buy lower to have the bigger gains, you also don't want to put up too much money that takes funds away from other sectors you wanted to invest in.

Large Pay Ratios are Another Red Flag

Anything above 100 percent translates into the company sending out more than they are making, an unstable practice.

This isn't the Casino

You are playing with real money, which is probably the only similarity. Those flashing tickers are not the same as the lights from the slot. Good investments should be boring.

Short-Term Means Higher Taxes

If you sell a stock within a year, then there is an additional capital gains tax that is larger than the long-term capital gains tax.

Set Emotions to the Side

Don't let how you feel about certain companies or sectors be an influence and prevent owning a diverse portfolio.

Keep Investments in U.S.

There are stock options overseas, but they usually come with additional taxes while also receiving some calls for the Internal Revenue Service.

Plan for the Long-Road

You can't make millions in a single day, nor could you make it from Seattle to New York in one day while driving. Patience is a virtue in both, as is dividend investing.

Reinvest Your Returns

Going back to the power of compounding, it's always a good idea to put what you earned back into your existing shares, or to buy additional ones to add more to your portfolio.

Be Consistent

While you are keeping an eye out every quarter, you'll want to expect your decisions to last for a good amount of years and not just a "New York minute."

Don't React Right Away

Even if a stock has a small drop in its value, that doesn't mean that you should drop it right away. One bad quarter doesn't mean that the company is going to head towards bankruptcy – give it some time.

Avoid Having Too Much Diversity

There are plenty of people who do want to have a lot of options, but there is a chance you'll miss out on big gains through your successful stocks. It also increases equal chance of losses.

Keep it Professional

While keeping emotions out, don't fall in love with a company you are investing in. It will make the decision to sell their stocks a lot more of a challenge when they fall consistently.

The Past Can Be Beneficial

Using what has happened in the past is a good way of knowing what to expect when entering the world of dividend stocks. Just keep in mind that history doesn't always provide a path to guarantee success.

There are No Guarantees

Like what "Rowdy" Roddy Piper used to say back in the 1980s world of professional wrestling, "Just when you think you have all the answers, I change the questions." The stock market feels like that sometimes.

Be Aware of Everything

If you don't keep an eye on your portfolio, things can go wrong very fast and very unexpectedly.

Paralyzed to Analyzing has One Simple Solution

Do something because doing nothing won't move that needle in the other direction.

Believe in Consumerism

There will always be something for people to put their money into. Just keep an eye on what people are interested in these days and look for those dividend options.

Don't Be Overconfident

Believing the hype means that you may overlook the mistakes you may not realize you are making.

Learn How to Handle Fear

At the same time, don't let it prevent you from making investments. That's why you do plenty of research ahead of time so that you make a good amount of funds.

Do You Stocks Have Good Marketing

Do people know the names of the companies you have in your portfolio. At least you can hope that doing a Google search helps find more than random results.

Avoid the "Rule of Three"

A lot of the mature companies begin to have similar characteristics after a long period of time, so you want to make sure you don't fall under the overplayed and overinvested.

Beware of Those Young Companies

They can easily go out of business or declare for bankruptcy after a few years. It's usually a good idea to wait more than five years before deciding.

Dividend Growth Investing is Not Unbeatable

While those are oftentimes a recommended investment option, they can always have a few flaws and require attention on the different valuations.

Remember a Loss Hurts More

In a lot of ways, a 75 percent loss requires having to gain a 300 percent gain just to break even.

Don't Try to Invest in the Next Big Thing

Consistency usually works well enough. You don't have to find the newest game-changing innovation.

Anyone Can Succeed

You don't have to be an "expert" with decades of experience. The biggest thing is education and having knowledge of the market.

The Tortoise Beat the Hare

"Slow and steady wins the race" also works when you are investing in dividend stocks.

Conclusion

It's safe to say that there's a reason that dividends are very popular among the investment community, and if there were a perfect way for them to work, it would be the slow and steady approach – rather than the one where the investor is hoping to find one big gold mine.

There are plenty of options and because the market offers plenty to choose from, it's a big reason why so many investors will establish a diverse portfolio. Those are the two main keys to success for the investor who is about to get started in the world of dividend investing.

Those who can plan accordingly and not be too hasty in their decisions to sell stocks at the slightest inkling of a decline, there are big rewards that await the investor who hopes to have enough money at the end of a few good decades of decisions – which will yield a dependable income to enjoy when you are retired from the workforce.

All it takes are solid decisions and being patient long enough to let them come to fruition.

Finally, we've now reached the end of this short book. After writing on the essence and mechanics of dividends and investments, one thing that sticks to my mind is the beauty of breaking free from the rat race of a rigid income, without making much impact. Investments give you the ability to decide how your life will turn out to be. It is beyond the circumstances of birth, race or social class! Your dream of becoming what you want to become is at the other side of investments. Warren Buffet only had a million dollars' worth of stocks in 1962. Today, he is one of the wealthiest men alive. You might not have a million dollar of stocks in your portfolio. Heck, you might not even have up to $1,000. The important thing is to keep your eyes fixated on the dream and work towards achieving it by harnessing the power of compound interests and investments. Mind you, I am not saying you will become rich overnight. Keep dreaming, and never let your dreams fade away. And remember, don't procrastinate - start early! As a matter of fact, start now!

CPSIA information can be obtained
at www.ICGtesting.com
Printed in the USA
LVHW052020131220
674086LV00033B/1100